BREAKING AND ENTERING

T0315955

by the same author

COLD MOUNTAIN

BREAKING AND ENTERING

Anthony Minghella

faber and faber

First published in 2006
by Faber and Faber Limited
3 Queen Square, London WCIN 3AU

Typeset by Country Setting, Kingsdown, Kent CT14 8ES
Printed in England by Mackays of Chatham plc, Chatham, Kent

Breaking and Entering © Anthony Minghella, 2006
Introduction © Anthony Minghella and Timothy Bricknell, 2006

Anthony Minghella is hereby identified as author
of this work in accordance with Section 77 of the Copyright,
Designs and Patents Act 1988

A CIP record for this book
is available from the British Library

ISBN 978–0–571–23646–6
0–571–23646–4

2 4 6 8 10 9 7 5 3 1

CONTENTS

INTRODUCTION

Anthony Minghella in conversation with Timothy Bricknell

Almost twenty years ago, in a period when I was in thrall to the seductions of Magical Realism, I wrote a short screenplay called *The Table* which was about a couple who had ordered a table from an immigrant carpenter at an extraordinarily cheap price. They ordered the table in ash with hand-carved decoration made to measure for a peculiar alcove in their kitchen. The Brazilian carpenter (also the boyfriend of their au pair) turns up with this beautiful table which slides perfectly into the alcove. The couple are absolutely delighted. They had commissioned the table for £150, but when the husband starts to write the carpenter a cheque, the carpenter demands cash. Although the couple worry that they don't have enough cash on them (which of course they do, but don't want to be cleaned out for the weekend) they eventually agree, although 'it is not how things are done in England'. But then the carpenter says he wants £250. 'You can't do that, Antonio, we've already shaken hands on £150 – you can't suddenly change the price.'

'But,' says the carpenter, 'it's a hand-carved table made to measure for your alcove!'

'Yes, but we've agreed a price and you can't change it. That's not how things are done over here.'

As they continue to squabble, the wife turns on the husband accusing him of being weak in negotiations. The husband protests that if they'd ordered a made-to-measure hand-carved table from someone else then they'd expect to pay ten times as much: £250 is still a good deal. During the squabble the carpenter pulls the table out from the alcove to take it away but, when the £250 is eventually paid, he leaves the table in the middle of the room and walks out.

Relieved and left alone, the couple try to put the table back in the alcove – but it doesn't fit. They turn it around, but it still doesn't fit. They turn it around again and it doesn't fit. In fact, it's getting bigger. The film finishes with the table growing in the middle of the room.

I was reading, like everyone else, many Latin and South American writers – Marquez, Borges, Allende – but, more importantly for me, it was making Jim Henson's *Storyteller* series that encouraged an interest in ideas that pushed narrative away from the hyper-naturalism which dominated everything at the time – including my own writing. *The Storyteller* had reminded me that when I was a child I had had an obsession with fairy tales. I had exhausted the library's collection of folk and fairy tales. I'd devour all these English, Norse, Irish, Jewish, Italian, Latin American parables, folk or fairy tales. I was a very precocious reader. My school career exhausted itself by the time I was about nine years old and then spiralled into complete decay.

I planned to write a whole series of short films – moral fables – along similar lines to *The Table*. It was going to be a twelve-part series called *Cuts, Stings and Bruises*. The second play I started writing was called *Breaking and Entering*, this time about a couple who come home after a dinner party to discover their house has been ransacked. When they come to do an inventory of what has been taken they discover, to their surprise, that things have actually been added. Somehow, what has been added is emblematic of the absences in their marriage . . . I could never properly write this idea, however, and I began work on another kind of film which became *Truly, Madly, Deeply*. Also very much a Magical Realist idea, *Truly, Madly, Deeply* began with the premise of what happens if you miss somebody so much that you cannot live without them, but, if they come back, can you really live with them? *Cuts, Stings and Bruises*, however, went away and the couple of notebooks I had scribbled notes in for *Breaking and Entering* got put in a drawer.

*

When I was making *Cold Mountain* I began to feel that if I didn't write an original screenplay for my next film then I would probably never write one again. It had been fifteen years since I had last written one. So, in my mind, I committed to making an original film and I decided that it would be contemporary and set in London. I thought that would lend the piece spontaneity and that I would avoid the enormous restrictions of period drama where everything has to be preordained and researched.

We renovated some offices in North London a few years ago. I'd acquired a small old chapel in an area that, as my son told me at the time, was 'not a good place for an office'. But I was stubborn about it and the building was beautiful. But, sure enough, our renovation work soon attracted the attention of socially excluded lads from the large surrounding housing estates. Whilst I was away scouting locations for *Cold Mountain*, a rosary of break-ins began. However minor the burglaries were, they became so frequent that the staff in London became quite demoralised, provoking sometimes quite hysterical reactions. In the process of dealing with the break-ins, we encountered some very interesting things. We met a CID detective who was extremely liberal and politicised in his views on petty crime and who felt strongly that, in his experience, the conventional method of dealing with offenders was not working. We also experienced Camden's experiment with ideas of conciliation – creating opportunities for those who were victims of crime and their perpetrators to encounter each other in a way that would prove salutary to the offenders and instructive to the victims: the story of the crime reflected back onto the perpetrator, so that that person personally encounters the effects of what they have done.

One of the characteristics of crime, of course, is that it does not want to contemplate the human cost or any human dimension to the activity. It is defined by anonymity. The idea of the conciliation scheme is that, for a criminal, really to encounter the pain caused by his actions can be as important a deterrent as being punished. Equally, there's a hope that if the person who has suffered from the crime can meet the perpetrator, then the crime will be contextualised differently and the trauma of it may be softened. The aim is to humanise an anonymous, traumatic, offensive event. Often, suffering a crime will activate a person's prejudices and they'll start to create a script of who may have committed the crime – a script which will reflect their prejudices and fears. In the conciliation meeting those prejudices of the victim are inflected by someone real, who almost never corresponds to the supposition.

When all this was happening to us, I was reminded of my notes for *Breaking and Entering* which I had never been able to write all those years ago. It occurred to me that the issue of conciliation and of trying to find out the truth behind a crime could be a very rich area to patrol, particularly because it corralled my desire to write about London. It seemed to offer the opportunity to cut across social boundaries and the hermetic nature of most of our inter- actions. Most people in a city encounter others from their own social territory and not their geographical one. This idea for a narrative device would allow me to trespass into many different territories.

The first page of notes I made on this project (and I kept all my notes for this project – curious to see how it began and where it would end up) is creased down the middle, divided into two parts: at the head of each part are the names of women. I wanted to organise the material around two mothers and two children. Both mothers, I decided, would be alone and both children would be special and demanding. At a schematic level, I was intrigued by how social opportunity affects the solutions people find to manage their lives and by the political connotations of that. Sometimes we treat people inhumanely and are then astonished by their inhumane actions; sometimes we reduce the options for people and then hold them in very poor regard when they behave poorly. It is much easier to be kind in kind environments and kind circumstances. Cities are the single clearest gesture of civilisation and the clearest indication that the state of our civilisation can be read in the state of our cities. They are severely dysfunctional but we continue to work on them, to try and improve them. We co-exist without much regard or knowledge of each other. The lack of community in London is very pronounced – we share the same geographical space without sharing any other aspects of our lives; we often don't share language or culture or even the same ideas of what it means to be Londoners. We have no way of knowing if we have anything in common with our neighbours. Every city has a million stories, the cliché goes, and London has several million. My interest in the nature of cities and the actual planning of them led naturally to choosing architecture as the profession of one of the protagonists.

Although contemporary and set in London, every part of *Breaking and Entering* was a departure for me and required just as much research as my period films. The story focuses on the two pages of the *A to Z* I can navigate better than any other place in the world, my most familiar mental geography, but I kept discovering how little I did actually know about what was going on; the social matrix; the realities of crime and policing it; how the criminal justice system works. I also had no idea what it means to have a child with some form of autism; or what it means to be a refugee from Bosnia; or what it means to be a free-runner. And I know very little about what architects actually do, or what a big scheme like the King's Cross redevelopment involves. At almost every juncture of the story I had to stop, go away and research before I could continue writing. The film became very complicated to write. I believe in everything being exactly right on the page, otherwise your story can quickly disintegrate. It wasn't long before I found myself listening to someone tell us that we had got the nationality of the prostitutes around King's Cross wrong and what they charge. Obviously, my research was not thorough enough! However, that goes to show the level of interrogation the film goes through when put in front of an audience.

The exciting part of writing *Breaking and Entering* was that there was no obvious destination. The great comfort of adapting a novel is in knowing that its design and its characters please people sufficiently for it to have been deemed worthy of the amount of money involved in turning it into a movie. If you're creating an original screenplay you have none of that security – though the corollary of that is that there is no prescription for where you are allowed to go. It is slightly terrifying because you have no means of knowing whether what intrigues you as a writer will intrigue anybody else. All I could do is test it out on the people around me and see if they were as exercised by some of the issues that the film rehearses as I was. For example, in no particular order: in a disposable society where we no longer need something to be worn out before we replace it, what is the real value of possessions? Does the diminished value placed on possessions translate to our emotional life? Are we encouraged to move on from a relationship when it ceases to be as attractive or exciting as the possibility of a new relationship that presents itself? Has that consumerist obsession so agitated our inner lives that we find it very difficult to stay inside a partnership? And how does the idea of marriage still apply in a society where there is no necessity to being married other than convention? Why do we place so much value on our 'things'? Are 'things' a provocation? Who do they really belong to? Is the crime in 'things' about their being taken or in the exploitation involved in their being made? These visible and invisible crimes interested me a great deal. I wanted to extemporise on that theme so that, at the end of the movie, the least guilty person is the person who is notionally on trial.

The theme of repair was also very important to me. When I was a young man I had an accident and was left with some scar tissue. I remember the surgeon telling me not to worry as the scar tissue was much more robust than my normal skin. I was always intrigued by the idea that the repaired part would be stronger than the undamaged part. That seemed like a good metaphor for a relationship, or at least an idea to be examined through a relationship. I wanted to look at the notion of 'second chances' – giving the criminal a second chance, giving the damaged woman a second chance, giving a relationship a second chance – to examine all the places where trying again might be preferable, in the end, to disposing of something or somebody.

Originally, my sense was that this film would be comic or picaresque in some way. I think you can still feel that in some areas. I wanted there to be a compassionate energy, beyond the comedy, that would take you through the movie, leading eventually to a place of non-judgement. Rather than reverting to prejudice, I wanted that prejudice to be examined and found to be inaccurate and misplaced. If we were able to know more about the collisions we have in our lives, then we would judge less and find it easier in our hearts to forgive each other. Like all Catholics, of course, I'm often reminded of prayers I had to learn, and here the Lord's Prayer – 'Forgive us our trespasses and help us forgive those who trespass against us' – was like a running rhyme through my head whilst I was writing.

When I started the first draft, the only destination I had in mind – other than the two women and children – was that a crime somehow leads a man from one relationship to another. The story would take him into a different social territory. And I wanted to include a court scene as I was very taken with the idea of the conciliation process. But I didn't want to know more than that. I didn't know, for example, that Will and Liv were not married. I don't think it helps, on a first draft, to have already mapped out the choreography of the events to the extent where there is nothing to be surprised by and the characters have to behave inside the shape you've made. Obviously, what happens through subsequent drafts is that you try to clarify and make necessary the structure that you've discovered and, if you can't, then you have to change it. I'm never frightened of unravelling anything but, initially, I want to find out, as organically as I can, who needs to be where for the story to make sense. I start at the beginning, write to the end, and then start at the beginning again. Certain things stay unchanged through ten or twelve drafts and many things are completely abandoned. In this screenplay, for example, many of the Amira and Will scenes are almost unchanged since the very first iteration of the screenplay – especially the sequence where Will first goes to Amira's apartment, the scene in the bedroom with Robin where he's trying on suits and the next couple of scenes with Amira.

I won't begin a first draft until I have a very clear idea about all of the characters. I can't write a scene by itself in isolation. I can't start to write and then discover what I'm writing about. It can take me months till I can write a scene. But I have to forgive myself for the way that I work. If I try to write the way I think a proper writer should, then I can't make any headway. However, once I get started I can write very quickly because by this point I know the characters well – I know what they do, what they've done, and what they want. But neither am I omniscient, and there's much to be discovered along the way. I'm often taken by surprise. For example, I didn't know that Amira was going to take the photographs until I was writing and then it seemed like the obvious thing to do. I had thought that the sexual relationship was going to be the thing which complicated and clouded the relationship between them – that Will would become so compromised that he was no longer able to prosecute his interest in Miro. But it seemed absolutely inevitable that she would come up with some insurance policy and do something so distasteful because of the strength of her determination to protect her son. She is also risking her happiness, because I think she is very invested in the relationship with Will. It is a genuine love affair – she is so unused to the kindness he shows towards her and he is so unsettled by her witnessing of him, her directness. One woman is incapable of a spontaneous action whilst the other is incapable of anything other. Liv is so distant and Amira so present. But, with Liv, her distance has been learned and is not innate – she has clearly been capable of great fire in their past. But it is a fire that has been extinguished by the burden of worry about her daughter, and by lack of sleep. Liv, I feel, has defined the terms of their relationship from the beginning. She's extremely controlling. Her personality needs – her melancholy, her disquiet, her obsession with the needs of her child, her indifference to Will's concerns about his work – seem to be the defining characteristics of their relationship. Intermingled, of course, with real pleasure and partnership, as well as Will's efforts to be a father to her daughter. But it is a relationship that does not take much stock of Will's needs.

It is not my intention to say that what Will does at the end of the film is correct in terms of being faithful to his 'marriage'. He confronts what he wants and that is to stay in his marriage, to make a marriage; he wants to smash the glass that seems to seclude Liv and Beatrice and make a relationship that he so often feels excluded from. That is what he wants more than the risk of going with Amira – but I am not trying to say that marriage is right and that flight from a marriage is wrong. At that moment that is the conclusion that Will reaches. When I wrote this screenplay I didn't know that that is how the film would end but I suppose I realised – in the same way that he realises – that he is in love with his partner. That is where he is most comfortable. I don't think there is anything wrong with that: part of the nourishment of a long-term relationship is in the time spent comforting each other. Part of what he understands of his relationship with Amira is that its exoticism and unlikeliness is both what fires it and what will ultimately destroy it: you cannot be in a strange relationship long before it ceases to be strange. It is so often the case that when a marriage breaks up because of an affair, the affair itself breaks up shortly thereafter. The affair is only defined by the marriage. Whilst I don't think the film makes any great advertisement for monogamy, I don't think it makes any great claims for the healing effects of adultery. All I am trying to illustrate is that, in this instance, the rupture in the relationship between Will and Liv will ultimately make it stronger. They are in a better place at the end than they are at the beginning. The chaos of the discovery of the affair enables a dialogue that would not have been possible otherwise, and they come to understand things about each other they have never had the chance to before.

The final version of the screenplay, which is published here, reflects the final version of the film. It differs from my first draft of the screenplay in two major ways. Firstly, it is shorter. An awful lot of material has gone, mainly from the beginning. It is pointless engaging in self-loathing, but it does make me crazy that no matter how many things I write, I never sufficiently trust the economy of film, I never sufficiently acclimatise to how little needs to be done before an audience knows where it is. I know it as a director but not as a writer. Almost all of the early establishing scenes have gone, or have been folded into montage. The second big change is in Will's personality. In my early drafts, Will was in a constant state of flirtation as I was trying to advertise his desire to be loved and to be wanted at a point where he was certainly not experiencing that at home. It was also a technique of his as a character, in his work, in his social behaviour – a technique that was not remotely an attractive characteristic but which made him attractive. Every encounter was a challenge and, although he wasn't involved in a hundred relationships, he loved the idea that he could be. The film, then, gave him what he wanted so that he could discover he didn't actually want it. The first of those opportunities is the collision with Oana – the opportunity to get laid with no consequences. I put Will in a car with a prostitute to ask, do you want this, and have him realise that, no, he doesn't. There was also a very attractive girl in the office whom he desired and whom he flirted with but, when he suggested they pursue the flirtation, she asked 'And then what?' 'And then we chase each other around the playground,' he replied – but his interest disappears, as he doesn't want to be thinking about the consequences of his actions. When the film offers him a real alternative to his life, in his relationship with Amira, he is terrified and out of his depth. And the consequences are calamitous.

I try to engineer a reverse prejudice or, at least, to offset judgement by introducing likeable characters you're not supposed to like so that you find yourself feeling sympathetic towards characters who may not normally be sympathetic. For example, the three main characters technically on the wrong side of the law are very likeable: Miro, the burglar, Oana, the prostitute and Amira – who does the most alarming thing in the film in terms of a moral transgression. At what appears to be the least appropriate moment, Amira has the presence of mind to take out an insurance policy to protect her son. But it is Will who probably commits the worst crime. As

Amira says: 'You steal someone's heart, that's a real crime' – however it's one that carries no punishment in our society but which can often cause the most damage. Similarly, there are other prejudices that surround the film. Will's business partner, Sandy, for example, will not engage with the dimensionality of what's happening: he simply sees that he's been robbed and so wants retribution. Sandy always takes the moral high ground, he is always certain: 'Except we haven't broken the law,' 'It's always about fooling around,' 'Don't exit fidelity,' 'He's going to prison.' Almost everything he says is certain, whereas almost everything that Will says, thinks and does is equivocal: so equivocal that he constantly uses metaphors to prevent the truth coming out in some naked, disagreeable way. He is so imprisoned by metaphor that he can't actually construct a sentence without employing it. It's a way of deflecting the truth about himself. The film wants to play with equivocations, moral uncertainties and prejudices.

The film asks who's at fault? And mostly, I think, nobody's at fault. It is easier to imagine that there are antagonists and protagonists – we make our fictions in that way, we tell our stories in that way. The good guys, the bad guys. We know, as we divide the world into good and evil, that it is a false distinction. 'There are three sides to every story: yours, mine and the truth,' the saying goes. I want to write in such a way as to discourage easy judgement, because it criminalises and marginalises people and causes enormous damage in our society. This has never been so manifest. We demonise each other on the basis of ideological differences, religious differences, racial differences, sexual differences. However it is a fact that we share so much more in common: we are all human, we are all vulnerable, we are all in need, we are all capable of good, and of evil. If the drama that we make does not reflect that, then what use is it?

One of the wonderful things about all dramatic narratives is that they offer this great opportunity to inhabit somebody else's point of view. Unfortunately, in life, if somebody behaves badly to you, you don't have the opportunity, always, to find out what they're thinking; similarly, if you have behaved badly you don't always have the opportunity to experience the consequences of your behaviour. Drama is like some kind of conciliation court in itself. It gives you the opportunity to see the trespassed and the trespasser experience their lives away from each other and together. Probably, if you look at any of my films where someone trespasses then the consequences are calamitous. Whether I like it or not, there is always this moral undercarriage. If you don't behave well in my stories, you'd better watch out.

New York, September 2006

PRELIMINARY NOTES FOR THE SCREENPLAY

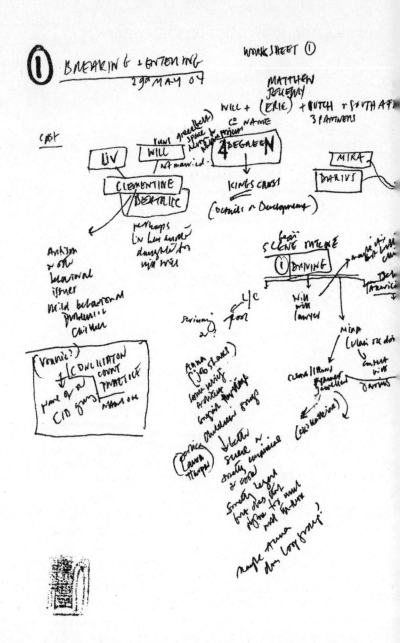

THEME OF PROPERTY
OWNERSHIP
THEFT
WILD v TAME

Frame
THADDEUS

a series of incidents, then.
what is the story

Man buys himself as a Meal
building secretly inspired
boy at the centre of the plot is brain
woman/mother of boy   complete devotion
sleeps with owner
getrude clemency
caricature court

Maria's girlfriend has
daughter Eleanor
who is disturbed
but a marvellous   swimmer
                    gymnast
                    athlete
                    violinist
Complete devotion
you can't understand complete devotion
and is also largely unmotivated

go on above?
what are the reasons?
what is the pleasure of
the top story?

This currently divides
a main story.
Goes again for the perspective
of the two more

eg: He leaves
and both women move in   one exchange
we make our point/below the move
                          the two children
Adoption?   She has a way
a kidnapping / is refusing to leave finally
                is one of the categories
                Her adverse will

(6)

BREAKING and ENTERING

9/8/04 @ The Dairy

- man buys building
- building gets broken into
- man discovers room burgled
- man catches burglar after many burglaries
- man seduces burglar's mother
- police called to interview
- burglar and man meet each other
- in conciliation court

How is the house
father in this story?
The children?
The work as opposed
+ the work place

The rhyme between
2 foreign women
are they gifts!
guilty children...

so need to pursue family.
pursue Davis
particularly i relation
+ his boys two other to
Bea...

Lead to pursue Bea, to Rafe
+ tensions us, and LIV
need to twist the accommodation
What's being stolen, by whom, from wh

Enter by the EYES and
not by the MOUTH

MILANI FLAT
- twosome
  Daniel + Milan

- THE CAR WASH   van with new computer

- THE EVENT? or more
  scene from physotherapist office
  (all these talk scenes seem
  too early now) owing scene
  with Liv and Bea is a therapist

○ The office,
     Sandy, cleaners, bill

○ The office
     not Break in. Interrupted, bill appears
     b/m return

○ Another morning after, but, clean? bill
     gets Maddaus

Sue knew of the
office at work

will return of the work
on service but
a intrusive att idea of
pronunciation Planning:
        → Serial
        → richer
     and Radical Architectural
            Vision, including
        the exploitation of public
     and green space

CAST AND CREW

Breaking and Emtering
was released on 10 November 2006

PRINCIPAL CAST

WILL	Jude Law
AMIRA	Juliette Binoche
LIV	Robin Wright Penn
SANDY	Martin Freeman
BRUNO	Ray Winstone
OANA	Vera Farmiga
MIRO	Rafi Gavron

PRINCIPAL CREW

Director	Anthony Minghella
Producers	Sydney Pollack
	Anthony Minghella
	Timothy Bricknell
Executive Producers	Bob Weinstein
	Harvey Weinstein
	Colin Vaines
Line Producer	Anita Overland
Cinematographer	Benoit Delhomme
Editor	Lisa Gunning
Production Designer	Alex McDowell
Music	Gabriel Yared
	Underworld

Breaking and Entering

INT. WILL'S CAR. KING'S CROSS. DAY

Will and Liv drive. There is an awkward silence between them. The atmosphere is charged.

> WILL
> (*voice-over*)
> When do you stop looking at each other? Shouldn't there be a warning? Shouldn't somebody say to us, 'Hey. Watch out. Pay attention.' Because you can be thinking, 'I'm okay. We're okay. We're good.' Then you turn around and there's this distance between you.

INT./EXT. KING'S CROSS DEVELOPMENT. MORNING

Europe's biggest construction site is seething with workers, spinning a web of metal as two ends of the new St Pancras Eurostar terminal inch towards each other. What's visible is impressive; equally convulsive is what's happening underground, where the vast infrastructure of tunnels, drains and underground track is being created. A huge mouth eating up Old London and spitting out New London in the form of station concourses, piazzas, hotels, residential buildings.

INT. KING'S CROSS DEVELOPMENT. ST PANCRAS BARLOW SHED. DAY

Will Francis's company, Green Effect, is one of the many companies whose name decorates the hoardings which enclose the development. He's taking a small group of MPs around the site accompanied by his partner, Sandy Hoffman. Green Effect is responsible for everything other than the buildings – all the public space, the landscaped space, the pedestrian flow, the traffic planning. Will explains in a theatre of gestures. It's much too noisy to have a conversation.

INT. BESPOKE HAND-CARWASH. KING'S CROSS. DAY

A deluge of water sluices the windscreen of the car in which Will and Sandy are talking. Outside men swarm around the car in overalls and galoshes, drowning the car, blasting it with water hoses, scrubbing at it, rocking it. Almost an assault. Some are African, some Eastern European.

The workers press in, faces close to the windows. One of them belongs to seventeen-year-old Zoran. The other to his cousin, Miro, fifteen.

EXT. WASTELAND NEAR CARWASH. DAY

A fenced area adjacent to the Carwash. It's private land but long a recreation area for the workers. Because there's so much demolition and development in the area, there's an odd sense of this being like a prison camp. Guys, still in their overalls, still wet, sit around smoking, taking their break. A game of football. Two teams, two colours: African; Eastern European. Miro and Zoran are playing.

The game grows in earnestness. The players shout at each other, in Nigerian, in Slavic languages. A heated tackle, the ball suddenly thrashed over a fence. Miro is called over. They know of his ability to climb. Zoran makes a chair with his hands and, effortlessly, Miro is up and over the fence. A second later and the ball flies up and over the fence. Another second and Miro reappears. With an acrobat's grace he drops to the ground and straight into a forward roll. During all this a red courier van, marked SPEED MERCHANT, has arrived. Some of the guys leave the game, stroll over to the Driver.

INT. SPEED MERCHANT VAN. DAY

The Driver has a map, his delivery documents. He's sharing these with the guys. Locates some photographs of the Sorting Station on his mobile phone. One of the men, Dragan, has a magazine and is looking up the computer models specified on the delivery documents, and sharing this information, too. They all point, discuss, compare and argue in heated Serbian. Finally, Vlado, dangerous-looking, a leader, and Zoran's father, slides open the door of the van.

Zoran! Miro!

Zoran looks up from the game, comes jogging over. Miro follows.

EXT. KING'S CROSS. DAY

The Speed Merchant van drives by this derelict area of King's Cross, passing through the debris and decay, en route to the Sorting Station.

INT. THE SORTING STATION. DAY

A large open space, girdled by galleries. The first floor has open-plan offices, the largest of which is shared by Will and Sandy.

There's a display area in the middle of the ground floor, with various of the company's competition models stacked in glass boxes, as well as a central location for an impressive model of Green Effect's contribution to the King's Cross project. In the model the development is enhanced by a whole series of interconnecting broadwalks and squares. Even more dramatic is the addition of a spur to the existing canal, creating an island around the development. The effect is quite severe and formal – lots of slate, lots of water, bridges.

The office is still somewhat unfinished: painters up on ladders, an electrician busy at some sockets. A great space but not slick. Basic materials – like a kindergarten for adults. Green Effect employs around twenty people. All look like architects, some of them are. Many are foreign, most of them young.

Tonight's the official opening. The joint is jumping.

Computer boxes are unpacked. The Speed Merchant Courier is having his docket signed. A Taiwanese girl, Wei Ping, beautiful, picks up a box and carries it up the stairs with Will.

A teenager, Bea, thirteen but looking younger, is here hanging large green balloons. Will's partner, Liv, is here, too, busy supervising the balloons. Liv is Bea's mother. She looks and sounds of Scandinavian origin. The balloons have Green Effect emblazoned on them.

INT. WILL AND SANDY'S OFFICE, SORTING STATION. LATE DAY

Sandy is setting up his computer.

> WILL
> (*notices the photographs on Sandy's computer*)
> Who's that?

> SANDY
> She's the cleaner, one of the cleaners, you know her. Erika.
> Staggering.

> WILL
> Sandy, why do you have a photograph of one of our
> cleaners on your computer?

> SANDY
> I was pretending I was experimenting with my camera.
> 'Oh hi, can I just try out my – click – thanks, seems to be
> working.'

EXT. CANAL SIDE OF SORTING STATION. LATE DAY

*Miro and Zoran jump down from a bridge over the canal. They look
over to see the Sorting Station.*

INT. WILL AND SANDY'S OFFICE, SORTING STATION. LATE DAY

> SANDY
> It's okay for you: gorgeous Swedish wife.

> WILL
> Girlfriend. Half-Swedish.

> SANDY
> You can't say girlfriend after ten years.

EXT. CANAL SIDE OF SORTING STATION. LATE DAY

*Miro and Zoran make a huge jump over a succession of rooftops,
leaping thrillingly into space. They arrive next to the Sorting Station.*

INT. WILL AND SANDY'S OFFICE, SORTING STATION. LATE DAY

> SANDY
> I mean is that true – you've been there – are you gassed in
> Sweden if you're ugly? Or just given a penis? Because the
> men can be very ugly, but I've never seen an ugly Swedish
> woman – look at Liv.

EXT. THE SORTING STATION. DAY

*Miro and Zoran watch through the skylights of the Sorting Station.
They see the comings and goings.*

INT. THE SORTING STATION. EVENING

*The party is in full swing. Everybody's in good cheer. Will and Sandy
make speeches. Guests jostle and mingle. Bea is climbing up the wall.
A concerned guest wants to reach out to rescue her. Liv intervenes.
Sandy is talking to Kate, an attractive female MP.*

EXT. THE SORTING STATION. NIGHT

*Will and Kate emerge into the cold night. She waves for her driver.
Headlights come on. Above them, standing on the roof of the adjacent
building, looking down, is Miro.*

> KATE
> I love this space.

> WILL
> We do. I think it's a steal. Take care.

*Miro watches as the Jaguar cruises up alongside Kate, and she slides
in. Will stands, enjoying the launch, king of his castle.*

EXT. KING'S CROSS. NIGHT

A fox crosses the road outside the St Pancras development.

INT. THE SORTING STATION. NIGHT

It appears to be hailing on the King's Cross model. Fragments of glass falling on the buildings. And then the warning note of the alarm, a countdown to it sounding.

Miro swings out of the rooflight, flips down and lands. He runs to the front door as the alarm ticks down, punches in the code. It doesn't work. He tries again. It stops just as the signal flatlines.

He pushes on the release mechanism of the fire door as Zoran and Dragan get out of a white van.

Miro opens some architecture books. Lots of photographs. He's going to take these. He examines the King's Cross model, picks up a handful of the model figures and heads for the door.

EXT. COUNCIL ESTATE. NIGHT

The white van draws up outside this modernist experiment in sixties public housing. Miro gets out, makes his way through the common and blighted walkways.

INT. AMIRA'S FLAT. NIGHT

Miro enters. The flat is quiet. Amira is asleep on the couch. The room is busy with her work, repairing, retailoring, making clothes, curtains. A tailor's dummy. A rail of clothes. An iron and ironing board permanently out. Miro glances in on his mother and then heads for the bedroom. Amira opens her eyes.

INT. MIRO'S BEDROOM. NIGHT

A man, a woman, a little girl – beautifully made figures. All on Miro's bed. He puts them on his bedside table.

INT. FRANCIS HOUSE, BEDROOM. NIGHT

Liv getting ready for bed. Will at the window.

WILL

Are we crazy?

LIV

No. About what?

WILL
(*buzzing*)
King's Cross. Sandy thinks we're crazy, to move there, to take on this project – but it's a great building, isn't it? It's a great project. And I thought it was a great night. I don't know.

LIV

It's all great.

He walks over to her at the dressing table, touches her.

WILL
Thanks for making the effort tonight. For the launch. I know it's not your . . . but it really helps.

LIV

It's okay.

WILL

Was it an effort?

LIV
What? (*Distracted.*) I think that's her. (*A little despondent.*) She was exhausted, I really thought . . .

WILL
No, that's a fox. They're taking over London. There'll soon be more foxes than people.

The fox screams.

I hate that noise.

LIV
(*she's already going away*)
No, it's Bea. I can hear her.

9

WILL

It's so late. How can she just not sleep?

She's leaving.

I don't think going to her, always, I don't know if that helps.

LIV

I know you don't.

WILL

I think we should go back and see someone, get some help.

LIV

I've seen too many someones. (*Leaves, returns immediately.*) Sorry. Don't worry about the building. It's wonderful. And what you're doing, the project, I think it can be something genuinely . . . (*Searching for the word.*) . . . genuinely –

WILL

(*prompting*)

Terrible? Rubbish?

LIV

Exactly. Genuinely terrible . . .

They kiss.

I'll come back.

And she exits.

INT. FRANCIS HOUSE, BEA'S BEDROOM. NIGHT

Bea does exercises on her beam. Barely any light. Liv stands in the doorway watching her.

LIV

Bea, darling, it's three-thirty in the morning. We have to stop this.

INT. FRANCIS HOUSE, BEDROOM. NIGHT

Will's getting into bed. The phone rings. Will picks it up. By the phone, photographs, happy times, Bea laughing, Liv and Will laughing.

WILL

Hello? Yes, well, no, I'm his partner, but – right, yes, we do, yes. What? When?

INT. THE SORTING STATION. NIGHT

Sandy walks past the flashing blue lights of a police car and into the chaos of the office. Officers are working, Will is talking to a female Police Officer, then sees Sandy.

WILL

All the computers, my laptop, the petty cash . . .

SANDY

How did they get in?

WILL

Through the roof.

SANDY

What about the alarm?

WILL

It was turned off.

SANDY

How did they know the code?

WILL

Sandy, I wasn't here, so I don't know.

PC PRIMUS

You have cleaners?

The guys nod.

SANDY

It's not the cleaners.

EXT. THE ARCHES, KING'S CROSS. DAY

Miro and Zoran are free-running along these Victorian arches, jumping walls. They swing over the wall and drop down to the lower level, tumbling into a forward roll by the lock-ups.

INT. VLADO'S LOCK-UP, THE ARCHES, KING'S CROSS. DAY

Dragan opens the door. Lets the boys in. The white van is parked outside. It's a warehouse of stolen goods, carefully organised. A façade of some other activity. Women in front of sewing machines and cutting cloth. Miro and Zoran go through the door at the rear and enter a room filled with electrical equipment: computers, TVs, stereos. Vlado is there.

VLADO

How's my best nephew?

He hugs Miro. Grabs his hands, shows them to Dragan.

See my hands, see his. His dad had the big brains, I had the big hands. (*To Miro.*) Your dad had hands like a girl's and the girls loved them. It's the same with you two. (*Of Zoran.*) My son is the clumsy one.

He goes to a shelf, pulls off Will's laptop. Hands it to a delighted Miro.

This is for you. Wipe everything. You know how to do that? Erase everything? Of course you do. They'll be delivering more computers and then you can go back in, my little monkey . . .

INT. AMIRA'S FLAT. DAY

Miro comes home, school uniform under a hoodie. Amira at the stove. She doesn't look up.

AMIRA

How was school?

MIRO

Okay.

AMIRA

Lot of homework?

MIRO

Not really.

AMIRA

Not really. Mirsad, you haven't been at school for weeks.
They sent another letter.

MIRO

It's a mistake. Half the time they don't know who's there,
who's not there.

AMIRA
(*going over, shaking him*)
Now we have to go back and see people at the Social
Services. We survived. Do you understand? We survived!
And that's not free!

MIRO

Get off me. I didn't ask to survive!

AMIRA

Look at me! Imagine your father. If we could offer him just
one day, one hour, imagine! (*Goes into Bosnian.*) And you
have your life, and what do you do with it?

MIRO

I don't even remember him, I don't remember him!

AMIRA

Where do you go? Where do you go every day?

MIRO

I'm working. I'm earning money.

AMIRA

You have to go to school. That's what we promised, with
the police, with the court. Otherwise they'll put you in
prison.

MIRO

I'll be sixteen in three months.

AMIRA

Mirsad, you're a clever boy. (*In Bosnian.*) You're clever.
You've got a brain.

MIRO

I have to go. I'm late.

AMIRA

If somebody, if one of his family, if any of our people, are leading you, I'm telling you – if any one of them is – I'll kill them. And I wouldn't care.

EXT. KING'S CROSS. DAY

Amira hurries through the crowds of people outside the station.

INT. BOSNIAN COMMUNITY CENTRE. NIGHT

An older man is calling Bingo in Bosnian. Two dozen people play the game. They munch snacks. Turkish coffee. Very smoky. Amira works at the canteen. She collects dishes. Listens to the Bingo Caller's mesmeric drone. Somebody wins. There's applause.

INT. AMIRA'S FLAT. BEDROOM. NIGHT

Bea is trampolining inside a computer screen. Miro has Will's computer on in the darkness of his bedroom, the screen lighting his face. Bea doing gymnastic work – she somersaults, she's on parallel bars, she's climbing. Miro considers her. Over these images of Bea:

LIV
(*out of shot*)

We've never really had a proper diagnosis, but I've always known that Bea was special. She's double happy, double sad, double excited, double awake, double needy – well, no, triple needy actually.

INT. PSYCHOLOGIST'S OFFICE. DAY

A Therapist's office, clearly involved with children, with puzzles, with drawings, a set of scales. A woman, Rosemary, is talking to Liv.

LIV

Even when Bea was ten months old, she was already distressed by noise. She would only sleep with a particular blanket or eat from a particular spoon . . .

EXT. BUILDING SITE, KING'S CROSS. DAY

A little hectic where building site and King's Cross pedestrian traffic collide. Too noisy to hear what's being said. A grim intersection. People living rough. Green Effect moving in behind the wire and notices. Will is trying to leave. He has an appointment. He's discussing something with the contractors. They want more information. He is desperate to extricate himself. Does so, drafting in one of his team to take over the explanation, then hurries away.

                    WILL
No, look, I'm sorry, I've got to. I'm late! I've got to go!

INT. PSYCHOLOGIST'S OFFICE. DAY

Rosemary is taking notes as Liv continues to explain . . .

                    LIV
She'll only eat foods of a certain colour.

Will hurries in.

                    WILL
Sorry.

                    ROSEMARY
                (brisk, not excusing)
I'm Rosemary McCloud.

                    WILL
Rosemary, I'm Will. Where is Bea?

                    ROSEMARY
Bea will – the structure is, I like to do a meeting with parents alone.

                    WILL
Great.

                    ROSEMARY
I'm just finishing with Liv. *(To Liv.)* I'd love to listen to some of these documentaries. I'm sure I must have heard them in the past.

LIV

They're mostly World Service –

WILL

Liv's explained she's gone into semi-retirement until Bea
gets –

LIV

That's not true –

WILL

Effectively. It's either Bea's gymnastics, Bea's art therapy,
Bea's music therapy – it's a sacrifice. Liv's won prizes for
her stuff, did she tell you that? It's a real sacrifice, is all I'm
saying. She's up all night.

LIV

I was explaining to Rosemary, these past few months, Bea
has been getting worse – she's really not sleeping or – it's
intense.

ROSEMARY

Have you had any history, yourself, of electing to see a
therapist or ever thought about it . . .?

LIV
(*a beat*)

I did see someone.

WILL
(*astonished*)

When?

LIV

I can get low. I've had low –

WILL

Wow!

LIV

My father died. My mother died. My sister died. It's a
family with a short life-expectancy.

WILL

And a grandmother of ninety-three . . .!

LIV

And a grandmother of ninety-three. Some days my cup is
empty, some days it's ninety-three full.

ROSEMARY

You were brought up in Sweden?

LIV

But my father was American. I was in university there.

WILL

Chicago. Addicted to cold.

LIV

No.

ROSEMARY

Are you concerned about Bea?

WILL

I mean, sure, but you know, Liv is, she does so much
worrying there's not much room for – but a thirteen-year-
old girl who collects batteries, who finds it hard to read,
who doesn't sleep, who doesn't let us sleep, who doesn't eat
anything, who wants to spend all day doing somersaults?
Sure I'm concerned. Of course I'm concerned.

ROSEMARY

Liv says you're wrapped up in your work.

WILL

Wrapped up?

LIV

That's fair.

WILL

I love the way working hard, working really hard, becomes
wrapped up, becomes something selfish. I love that. The
breadwinner is *wrapped up*, the breadwinner is –

LIV

C'mon, even getting you here –

ROSEMARY

When you say you love it, do you mean you don't love it?

WILL

Let's just back up. We love Bea. It's not a competition to
see who loves her the most. If it were a competition I'd be
happy to let Liv win. You win.

INT. FRANCIS HOUSE. BEA'S BEDROOM. NIGHT

*Liv sits on the floor in front of a SAD light box, feels the ultraviolet
on her face as Bea practises a back-flip. Again and again and again.*

LEGGE

(*out of shot*)

Says here your father died, your husband, your sister – and
this was where, in Sarajevo? You were all there?

INT. YOUTH OFFENDING TEAM HQ. LONDON. DAY

*A makeshift assessment room for this underfunded Agency. Kevin
Legge, a dour character, is interviewing Miro and Amira. Miro clearly
doesn't want to be there, is shrunk into his chair.*

AMIRA

Miro and I left with the Red Cross . . . my husband stayed
behind and was – he stayed behind and he was murdered.

LEGGE

You're Serbs?

AMIRA

My husband was Serb. I'm Muslim. It's complicated. We're
Bosnian. It's complicated.

LEGGE

And you have relatives, in Britain?

AMIRA

My husband's family. His brother. Sisters. An aunt.

LEGGE

Once upon a time, a smack around the ear or – My auntie
would give me a thump, matter of fact she punctured my
eardrum at one point, but you knew where you were.
Simple. We're all simple.

AMIRA

We need a bigger flat. That's a simple problem.

LEGGE
(*ugly*)

What about a suite at the Hilton? Jacuzzi? Me too. Camera
on your phone?

AMIRA

Just a bedroom for both of us.

LEGGE

What about you, Sunny Jim? What've you been up to when
you've not been at school? Back thieving? Stealing again?
Eh? See, things are not things. They're always somebody's
things. A car is Jack's car. He worked for it. Your Prada
jacket is little Kevin's Prada jacket and before it was his –
'cause I can see your brain ticking over – his Prada jacket
belonged to Mr Prada. A thing is always somebody's thing,
it's personal.

MIRO

What about before that?

LEGGE

Before what?

MIRO

Before it was Mr Prada's? Did it belong to the woman who
made it? 'Cause my mum does that, makes up clothes for
other people . . . slaves for other people. Or like when
prisoners make trainers.

LEGGE

Smart Alec. Next time you're getting sent down. We'll catch
you and then you can discuss who owns the trainers with
your cellmates . . . Back in a minute . . .

INT. THE SORTING STATION. LATE DAY

Sandy comes into the foyer, passing the Courier from Speed Merchant, who's having his docket signed. Sees Erika on her hands and knees sweeping up, nods to her. Some techies are reinstalling computers, new boxes open and everywhere.

INT. WILL AND SANDY'S OFFICE. LATE DAY

Erika appears, awkward.

> SANDY
>
> Come in. It's Erika, isn't it?

> ERIKA
>
> Yes, sir.

> SANDY
>
> Sandy.

> ERIKA
>
> We set the alarm, sir. I promise. I did it myself. You have my word.

> SANDY
>
> Hold on – I'm not accusing you.

> ERIKA
>
> The police already called my mobile phone, asking me questions.

> SANDY
>
> That's normal.

> ERIKA
>
> About this thing and that thing.

> SANDY
>
> I'm sorry.

> ERIKA
>
> It was like Kafka.

> SANDY
>
> Kafka?

ERIKA

It's like, 'Where did you get your car? Why are you ordering take-away?' We try to do a good job.

SANDY

And you do. You do. Are you a student of Kafka, then?

ERIKA

Not really. Why? Are you?

SANDY

No, no, I'm not. Erika, listen, we have to have a new code for the alarm. We're going to give you your own code, you're going to choose it, not us, so there's no chance you could ever be wrongly accused of anything . . .

ERIKA

Okay.

SANDY

I had your photograph in my other computer. What would the burglar have made of that?

ERIKA

My photograph?

SANDY

Only because when I was trying out my camera, remember? So a burglar who wouldn't know the context, they'd think you were a friend, or a girlfriend, or – like right now, somebody looking through the window, who couldn't hear, what would they think?

ERIKA

Apart from my uniform . . .

SANDY

Sure. No, sure, but say we were too far away to see the uniform, and then, I don't know, say I gave you – (*Grabs a book.*) – this book, for all the matey boy out there would know could be the *Collected Works of Franz Kafka*, it could be your birthday –

Or the Bible.

SANDY

Or the Bible. That's right.

INT. AMIRA'S FLAT. BEDROOM. NIGHT

Miro is on Will's laptop. He's looking through Will's photo library. He inserts a CD and burns the photographs onto it.

INT. FRANCIS HOUSE. NIGHT

A small aquarium. Fish swim in foreground. There's some kind of commotion. Liv and Bea in debate, at odds about something. Will on the phone, in a tussle with Sandy.

LIV	BEATRICE
When I said play with your fish, I didn't mean, that's not the same thing as – they can't breathe when they're out of the water. No, darling, don't, you can't put them back in, it's too late and –	I didn't do anything to them, you said play with them, I just took them out to look at them, I didn't hurt them, I don't know why they're not swimming. If I put them back in again . . .

During this Will walks in and out of shot, occasionally distracted by what's going on in the room, then back to the phone:

WILL

I don't understand though – Why do they need it again? No, we haven't changed the model, no, because then that's another planning round, and we'll never start the – not one email, about fifty emails! – I don't have my laptop, Sandy, it was stolen – (*To Bea.*) No, darling, not the, it's too late, listen to Mummy – (*Back to Sandy on phone.*) Sorry, no, nothing, no, it's just I'll have to go back to the office. (*Listens.*) That would be great, Sandy, sure, if you could go, then I could stay and help here . . . Brilliant.

EXT. THE SORTING STATION. NIGHT

It's dark. The Cleaners are leaving, turning off lights. Somebody is watching them. It's Miro, wedged into a gully, high up in the rooftops. He has binoculars and raises them just in time as Erika punches in the new code, teaching it to her partner. She's mouthing it – '2178' – then punches it in. Miro writes it on his hand. Below, the Mercedes backs out of the lane. A few seconds later and the white van backs in.

Miro has levered open the side vent of the rooflight. He squeezes into the unlikely gap and drops through.

INT. THE SORTING STATION. NIGHT

Miro runs through the building, alarm warning buzzing. Arrives at the alarm, punches in the cleaners' code, opens the fire door. Zoran walks in. They turn on the lights.

INT. THE SORTING STATION, OUTSIDE WILL AND SANDY'S OFFICE. NIGHT

Zoran emerges from Will and Sandy's office with a large flatscreen monitor, grins at Miro who passes him on his way back into the office. Miro produces a CD-ROM from his hoodie, puts it on Will's desk.

> ZORAN
> Now what you doing?

INT. DOWNSTAIRS AT THE SORTING STATION. NIGHT

Miro passes the model, can't resist, pockets some more of the figures. A horn blasts sharply, three times. Zoran drops the computer he's carrying as they both dash for the door.

EXT. THE SORTING STATION. NIGHT

The van is already moving. Miro and Zoran dive for the back door as a car comes towards them. The van hits the side of the car and skids away. Sandy gets out of his car, confused and in disarray. He can't read the licence plate of the van, nor see clearly in the badly lit

alleyway. He approaches the building, its door open, the computer
abandoned, innards exposed from the drop.

INT. THE SORTING STATION. MORNING

Will comes down the stairs towards Detective Bruno Fella, CID, who
stands poring over the King's Cross model, coffee in hand.

> BRUNO
>
> This is brilliant. You're really going to do all this? Put a
> canal right through the middle? It's like Venice. Brilliant.
> I'm Bruno. Detective Bruno Fella. CID. Are you Sandy or
> Will?

> WILL
>
> Will.

> BRUNO
>
> Hello, Will. I was born there. Just about there. (*He prods the*
> *model.*) I would have drowned. I love it. I think it's really
> nice . . .

> WILL
> (*as Sandy joins them*)
> This is my partner, Sandy Hoffman.

> BRUNO
>
> Sandy? Detective Bruno Fella. Just saying, fabulous
> building.

> SANDY
>
> Thanks.

> BRUNO
>
> Was it you had the scrape with the villains?

> SANDY
>
> I don't know about a scrape. They scraped my car. I was
> running late for the first break-in, not quite prepared for
> the second.

> BRUNO
>
> No, I completely get it. You're disgruntled. I would be.

Gone to all the trouble to make a fabulous building in a hostile community, last thing you want is all this grief.

SANDY

It's no fun. Financially it's a disaster. The insurance will be through the roof . . .

BRUNO

I tell you what your problem is, King's Cross, which is – what is it? We've got you, the British Library, we've got Eurostar, but we've also got crack village, we've got Somalians with machetes – it's an area *in flux*.

WILL

They left a computer disk, the burglars, did you know that? With my photographs . . .

BRUNO

What do you mean, they left it where?

WILL
(*holding it up*)
No, they returned it. More than that, they downloaded my personal photographs from my laptop, which they stole last time, and left it on my desk.

BRUNO

So can we see it? So they've got compassion.

WILL

I wouldn't go that far.

BRUNO

Not saying you have to have compassion for them. That's what my girlfriend says. My ex-girlfriend. They're the criminals. They're the bad guys. (*Handing back the disk.*) Can I see?

Will goes to a computer, calling up iPhoto.

Gotta love the Mac, eh? Sweet.

WILL

And what do you say to your girlfriend?

25

BRUNO

I'm the Old Bill, Will. I've been on the beat, I've been
undercover, I've been in a suit. The law, it's Einstein's law
of relativity.

WILL

Which means what, exactly?

BRUNO

It means relatively speaking, you and me, we break the law,
we get a decent lawyer. Now these guys that broke in here
it's 'Go Straight to Jail, Do Not Pass Go' . . . One law for
us, one for them.

SANDY

Except we haven't broken the law.

BRUNO

Everyone's broke the law.

INT. AMIRA'S FLAT. BEDROOOM. NIGHT

*Miro is looking at Will's laptop again. He's taking the virtual tour of
the King's Cross project, accompanied by Will's voice and intermittent
image.*

WILL
(*on computer screen*)
Our vision for King's Cross, for the public spaces of King's
Cross, starts with the premise that we acknowledge that
an urban landscape is a built landscape; starts as an
argument with Society's phoney love affair with Nature . . .
We are against the mistaking of grass for nature, of green
for nature . . . King's Cross is an area of North London
associated with poverty, crime, vice and urban decay.

INT./EXT. KING'S CROSS DEVELOPMENT. DAY

*The work continues in King's Cross. Welders weld; cranes crane;
builders build.*

WILL
(*out of shot*)

Our job is to transform the landscape, not decorate it with green, because how we think about ourselves, how we behave, is directly affected by the space around us. How we design the outdoors of our city is as important as how we design the indoors. We're going to take the canal and use it like calligraphy, like ink, to write around the development . . .

EXT. KING'S CROSS, WASTELAND NEXT TO CARWASH. DAY

Green Effect group gather inside a temporary canteen area. Will takes off his hard hat, sips at a coffee. His team around him. Apprehension in the air. A deputation.

JOE
We think it's the cleaners.

WILL
What about the cleaners?

JOE
Breaking in.

ORIT
They don't even clean properly.

RUBY
It's true. They don't. They never empty the dishwasher, or load it.

ORIT
They bring their kids and their boyfriends.

WILL
C'mon!

ORIT
They do!

JOE
They're cleaners and they're not clean.

27

WILL
(*putting on his hard hat*)
Okay. Good. Thanks. Thanks for the coffee. Thanks for the theory.

JOE
I'm sorry, but what does that mean?

WILL
It means your boyfriend's been at the office, Ruby, and yours, Wei Ping, and yours, actually, Joe, so where do the rules say we can have boyfriends, but the cleaners can't, or kids? And explain to me, please, how the cleaners are getting up onto the roof and then swinging through the roof-light and why they are when they already have keys and the codes.

During this, Sandy's driven up. Will goes to him.

I'm trying to defend the cleaners.

SANDY
So I just spoke to the alarm company. Whoever broke in used the cleaners' code.

EXT. INSIDE SANDY'S CAR. OUTSIDE SORTING STATION. NIGHT

Sandy's car parked in the alley. Sandy and Will inside. Lights are on inside. Sandy has binoculars and trains them around the building.

WILL
What do we do if we actually see a burglar? Call the police? Kill them?

SANDY
There's a weird ecology, of course, to these burglaries. The new computers, they're upgrades. They're new models. You could argue a break-in every six months, say, is good business . . .

WILL
Just not every six days.

28

SANDY

I wish somebody would steal this car, for instance. Forty-two thousand miles . . .

WILL

I've got the criminal mind. Lots of wanting to be bad. See an arse, want to bite it. I just never do.

SANDY

Good. We've strayed now from the criminal to the moral. We've crossed the criminal/moral divide. Wanting to bite an arse, that's a moral issue, and then only if the arse belongs to somebody who's opposed to the idea. Criminal would be biting an arse without permission.

WILL

You're such a lawyer! Anyway, and then what?

SANDY

Then what what?

WILL

You bite the arse and then what?

SANDY

Then they bite yours, is the theory. It's so long since I've bitten or been bit. (*He thinks on this.*) Good to talk, though.

Will nods.

Problem is, you find out we're all so miserable.

A cyclist goes past the car. It's Yakubu, Erika's boyfriend. He rings the bell of the Sorting Station. Will and Sandy slump down in the seats. Erika appears. Sandy and Will can't hear what's being said. Sandy watches through binoculars.

He's not happy.

WILL

You recognise him?

SANDY

No. Wish I could lip-read. I think I can! 'I – don't – like – you any more. I like Sandy. He's everything I want – in a man. And stop burgling his office.'

Sandy slumps down again as Yakubu cycles by. Erika watches him go, then shuts the door. They settle up in their seats again. A sudden knock on the door is shocking and they both jump. It's a woman, in a fur coat, clearly a prostitute. Will winds down the window. Her name's Oana.

OANA

Got a light?

WILL

Sorry. We don't smoke.

OANA

There's a car lighter.

WILL

Right.

OANA

I've got nothing on under my coat.

WILL
(*holding up the lighter*)
This isn't going to warm you up. Okay? Have a good night?

OANA

Can I get inside? It's cold.

SANDY

Whoa, this is a car, it's not a community centre. Jesus Christ!

But she's in. She fills the back seat with smoke.

OANA

So what are you guys looking for?

Another rap on the window. It's Erika. Irate. Sandy winds down the window.

ERIKA

Are you spying on us?

SANDY

Not at all.

OANA

Who's she?

ERIKA

It's insulting.

SANDY

No. Really. No insult intended.

ERIKA

If you don't trust us.

OANA

This your girlfriend?

SANDY

No.

WILL

No.

OANA
(*to Erika*)

Trust, if you have to say it, it means there is none. Use a condom. That's my answer to trust. 'Sure, I trust you. Use a condom.'

ERIKA

One minute you're nice to me, the next you're spying on me.

SANDY

No, Erika, listen.

He gets out of the car. Oana taps Will's shoulder.

OANA

Fifty pounds. Whatever you want.

WILL

What's your name?

OANA

Except talk. No talk.

                              WILL

What if I want talk?

                              OANA

Call the Samaritans. (*Sighs.*) Humans, we talk. Why?
Animals don't talk. Because they don't lie.

*The Mercedes roars past them. Sandy, conversation over, sidles back to
the car, gets in.*

                             SANDY

That was good. (*To Oana.*) You really helped.

                              WILL

We'd better lock up.

                              OANA

You work here?

                              WILL

Yeah.

                              OANA

Bad place for an office.

INT. AMIRA'S FLAT. EVENING

*Miro's working away at his project. Making a model of rooftops.
Amira has to go to work. She clears plates away, tidies up the
architecture books, considers them.*

                             AMIRA

It's funny. Your dada built bridges, but he always loved
buildings. 'Bridges can take you home, but buildings are
home.' That's what he said. What's your project about?

                             MIRO
                          (*honest*)
I don't really know. A place I'd like to live in. Or run
through.

                             AMIRA

I'd love to jump from building to building. Is it amazing?

                    MIRO
But what?

                    AMIRA
No buts. Is it amazing?

                    MIRO
Yes.

                    AMIRA
But dangerous? (*Stopping herself.*) No buts.

                    MIRO
You see the city.

                    AMIRA
What's it like?

                    MIRO
Better. (*Not looking at her.*) Did my dad just not want to
come with us?

                    AMIRA
                  (*floundering*)
He loved you. But he was needed. Every bridge was blown
up. It's complicated. No story from Sarajevo is simple.

EXT. FRANCIS HOUSE. STREET. EARLY EVENING

*Will gets out of his car, sees Liv at the window, her back to him. She's
in a fight with Bea. There's some kind of intense struggle going on,
with Bea in the grip of a fury. She knocks something over. It breaks.
Will watches, can't face going home. He drives away.*

EXT. THE SORTING STATION. NIGHT

*Another night. Will is watching the building from his car. He sees
a man emerge from the alleyway, closely followed by Oana who is
adjusting her skirt, she gestures 'Blah blah blah' at him.*

INT. FRANCIS HOUSE. KITCHEN. EVENING

A quiet table, Liv, Will, Bea. Liv serves chicken. Will eats a little, gets up, goes to the bread bin. Rummages around. Is confused.

WILL

There's no bread.

LIV

No bread. No butter. No flour. No dairy. Nor last night. You didn't notice.

BEATRICE

I did.

LIV

We're trying a diet. How's the chicken?

WILL

Chicken's good.

LIV

Bea? You going to try some?

BEATRICE
(*getting up*)

Ice cream is dairy.

LIV

Ice cream is dairy. Try the chicken. It's really good. Come on, Bea, this is a special diet just for you.

Bea is at the fridge.

Rosemary suggested we try this. Remember? Therapist Rosemary? Amazing stuff about food, about the effect of food on mood, on the brain.

WILL

Rosemary? She said that . . . Wow.

LIV

Every time I say something in this house, it gets repeated back as a question. I say good morning, people ask me what makes me think it's a good morning.

WILL

What?

LIV

I'm trying to hold this family together.

BEATRICE

No ice cream! There's no ice cream!

WILL

Who are 'people'? Who are these mysterious *people* who question whether it's a good morning?

LIV

You know, because I feel such a fool with my sun box, but it's the only sun you can rely on in this house.

WILL

Liv, what are you talking about? I just wanted a slice of bread.

BEATRICE

When I say I don't want food, you say eat. When I say I want food, you say don't eat. It's not fair!

LIV

Can't we just try this together as a family? For a week, for two weeks?

WILL

Don't say 'try together', that's all, if we don't decide together.

LIV

Don't say 'decide together', that's all, if we don't cook together, or talk together, or do anything together.

Bea starts to rock and make a droning sound, shutting them out.

WILL

Don't do anything together?!

LIV

There we are.

WILL

There we are what ?

LIV

You don't even hear it.

BEATRICE
(*on a loop*)
I have to go and exercise, I have to go and exercise, I have
to go and exercise . . .

WILL

Eat some chicken first.

BEATRICE

I'm vegetarian. Eating flesh is disgusting.

WILL

You don't eat vegetables!

LIV

Sweetheart, we know this, you get hyper, if you eat sugar,
you get a little hyper . . .

BEATRICE
(*knocking over the plate*)
It's disgusting! It's disgusting! No! No! No!

WILL

No, what we know is, we just have to shout and scream and
break a few things and we get our own way –

Bea is already leaving the room.

Or run away. Great.

Liv starts picking up the food, won't speak.

Liv. Liv. Liv! Or else just say nothing. Because God forbid
we ever said what we meant – no, just let's have the shutter
come right down! (*Claustrophobic.*) Anyway, I have to go
back to the office, so –

*As Will leaves, Liv goes to the bin, picks out the broken plate and
attempts to repair it.*

EXT. FRANCIS HOUSE. STREET. EVENING

Will emerges from the house, looks for his car, fishing out his car keys as he finds it. He presses the remote. Nothing happens. He examines the remote, pressing it. Nothing. He slides the fob. No battery.

INT. FRANCIS HOUSE. BEA'S BEDROOM. EVENING

Bea is in a headstand. Will enters. Watches her for a second.

> WILL
>
> Bea, my car keys, where's the battery?

She keeps vaulting.

> Bea.

She keeps vaulting.

> Hey!

His ferocity stops her.

> I need the battery. Don't punish us. We're human. We get fed up.

> BEATRICE
> (*confused*)
> Fed up? Is that about the diet?

> WILL
>
> It means upset. I don't know why, it's a metaphor. We talked about those, remember, 'cried your eyes out' doesn't mean your eyes fall out – metaphors, 'fed up'. It's not about food. Where's my battery?

Now Liv has appeared.

> BEATRICE
>
> In my box.

> WILL
>
> Where's your box?

> BEATRICE
>
> It's my box. You can't go in my box.

WILL

Then you go and get the battery.

LIV

Bea?

WILL

It's all right. We're working it out.

LIV

Bea, go and get Will's battery.

Bea is taken by this circumlocution. Goes out of the room.

WILL

Will's battery?

LIV

Can you explain to me why you suddenly need to go to the
office every night?

WILL

You know why.

LIV

You're not the police.

WILL

The police are not night watchmen.

LIV

Nor are you! Most wives would worry if their husbands go
cruising in King's Cross every night.

WILL

Come on!

LIV

Hire a security company!

WILL

Most wives are married to their husbands! As we're being
so accurate tonight. Dads. Wives. *Will's battery!* Thanks.
And I don't see much sign of the real father. (*He's leaving.*)
I love the sun box, whatever the fuck it's supposed to do.
I keep hoping it'll warm you up.

38

EXT. KING'S CROSS. NIGHT

Will drives through King's Cross. Passes the late-night revellers, the drunks, the homeless.

INT. WILL'S CAR, OUTSIDE THE SORTING STATION. NIGHT

Wipers clear the smatterings of rain. Will sits, watches the office. Oana appears, hugging two cups of coffee.

> OANA
>
> Skinny cap, extra shot, right?

> WILL
>
> Right. Thanks.

No words for a while. They sip the coffees.

> OANA
>
> I brought a CD.

> WILL
>
> I've got CDs.

> OANA
>
> No. For dancing. I like to dance.

> WILL
>
> In cars?

> OANA
>
> Or outside. It stops raining, I'll dance for you outside. Up to you. If you want I can dance on your lap. But that's not free.

> WILL
>
> Absolutely.

> OANA
>
> I still make you come, but not inside me. Some guys think that's not cheating.

She fishes out the CD. He puts it in. The music sounds. P J Harvey. Oana starts to dance in her seat. It's sexy. After a moment Will stops it.

WILL

That's good. You are, you're very good.

OANA
(*looking at him*)

That's okay. It's fine.

WILL

What do you mean?

OANA

It's okay.

INT. FRANCIS HOUSE. BEDROOM. NIGHT

Fox howls. Will slides into bed. It's very late.

WILL

Hi. I'm sorry.

LIV

You smell of perfume.

WILL

Well, I don't know how I do.

LIV

Nor do I.

He reaches out to her.

WILL

I love you.

LIV

Is that an answer?

WILL

It's the truth.

They lie there. The fox starts screaming.

What do you want? What do you need? Ever? I feel as if I'm
tapping on a window. That you're somewhere behind the
glass and you can't hear me. Even when you're angry with

me, like now, it's like someone a long, long way away being angry with me.

LIV

Well, glass, that's better than ice, which is where we were earlier. Sweden, ice, depression. The high rate of suicide. I never got close to anybody who didn't want to talk about that. Or free love. Or Liv Ullmann. Who's Norwegian.

WILL

That's because there are no other Swedes to talk about. Nobody lives there. You can drive for hours before you pass another Volvo. Abba. Let's face it. It's a sorry old list.

LIV

You're English! You've brought us what? Sarcasm? The Beatles! Yeah yeah yeah!

WILL
(sings)
'Knowing me, knowing you.'

LIV

Lager louts!

WILL

No, you invented lager.

LIV

Excuse me, the Danes!

WILL

Same difference.

They laugh. A thaw.

I love your laugh. I'd like to gather up all your laughs and lock them in a box, like Bea's, and nobody would be allowed the key.

LIV

Where are you going?

WILL

To shower.

LIV

Come back.

WILL

Or kill that fucking fox.

He comes back, lies on top of her, the cover between them. And then they kiss.

INT. FRANCIS HOUSE. BEDROOM. DAWN

First light. Liv's nightdress, discarded on top of the bed. Bea is trying to wake Liv who, for once, is fast asleep. Will turns over. He looks at the clock. 6.00 a.m.

WILL

I'll take you. I'm taking you.

BEATRICE

Mum takes me.

LIV

I'm getting up. It's okay.

WILL

I'm taking Bea. I want to. Go back to sleep.

Bea stares at the nightdress, appalled, as if it were a corpse lying on the bed. Will gets out from under the duvet.

BEATRICE

Mum takes me.

LIV

Daddy can take you today. It's fine.

WILL

See, I'm up.

EXT. FRANCIS HOUSE. STREET. EARLY MORNING

Will and Bea get in the car. He turns on the engine. Rap music blasts out. Will presses eject, fumbles with the CD.

BEATRICE

What's that? Is that a CD?

WILL

Yeah, it's a – yep, it's a CD.

BEATRICE

Is it yours?

WILL

Yep.

BEATRICE
(*impressed*)

Shut up!

WILL

Shut up? Is 'shut up' good? That's good, isn't it? Excellent.

He turns it back on.

INT. LEISURE CENTRE. GYM. EARLY MORNING

Bea working with Paul, her coach. She's really good. Will looks on from the viewing area in the café. He's working on some drawings, black book surrounded by buttered toast and marmalade. Bea does her routines. Will watches, enthralled. He waves. She sees him, waves back.

INT. LEISURE CENTRE. OUTSIDE CHANGING ROOM. EARLY MORNING

Will waits for Bea. She emerges in her school uniform. Bedraggled.

WILL

Sweetie, you're still wet. You're dripping.

BEATRICE

Yellow towel.

WILL

It wasn't yellow. Was it yellow?

BEATRICE

Yellow stitching.

43

WILL
You have to dry yourself.

BEATRICE
I did. I used the hairdryer.

WILL
You're soaked. What about my sweater? That's sort of a
towel. Is it a good colour?

BEATRICE
Colour is good. Sort of a towel. You'll be cold.

WILL
If I get cold, I'll wear the towel.

He pulls off the sweatshirt. She disappears back inside.

EXT. LEISURE CENTRE. PLAYGROUND. MORNING

*Outside, there's a playground area, close to the car park. Miro, Zoran,
a few others, are doing their free-running exercises, like circuit training.
Amira arrives, watches. She's astonished by Miro. His grace. He sees
her, nods shyly. She comes closer, hangs her coat on a branch.*

AMIRA
I want a lesson.

*The other boys are amused. She tries a move. Bea and Will come out
of the Leisure Centre. Miro makes a move. Amira tries to follow. Will
is intrigued. She's got a great laugh. Then she lands on her backside.
Miro helps her up. She's wet . . . Amira tries to dry herself. Will finds
the towel and approaches.*

WILL
We'd like to donate our towel.

AMIRA
I'm fine, thank you.

WILL
Truly. We hate our towel. It's looking for a new home.

BEATRICE
We hate our towel.

                    AMIRA
                  (*accepting it*)
    Thank you.

*Will and Bea head for the car. Amira dries herself, watching them go.
Miro teases her and she chases after him.*

INT. WILL'S CAR, OUTSIDE THE SORTING STATION. NIGHT

Will and Oana, drinking their coffee. Will winds down the window.

                    OANA
    It's cold.

                    WILL
    Yeah, it's a bit cold.

                    OANA
    Why wind down the window?

                    WILL
    Get some air.

                    OANA
    Why?

                    WILL
    You know. (*Pause.*) Quite a strong perfume.

                    OANA
    It's my job.

                    WILL
    Actually. I bought you a present. Sort of in return for the
    CD.

*He's rummaging around in the glove compartment and produces a
bottle of perfume from the glove compartment.*

    It's good. I think. My wife uses it. She says it's good.

                    OANA
    That's fucked up.

                    WILL
    Is it?

                      45

OANA

What man wants to be with a girl who smells like his wife?
Anyway, you think I like to smell like this, you think I like
to wear panties which cut my pussy in half?

WILL

Who said anything about –?

OANA

Men are incredible!

EXT. ROOF OF THE SORTING STATION. NIGHT

*Above their heads, perched on the roof of the office, Miro contemplates
the rooflight, now all boarded up. No way in. He pulls at the boards,
suddenly pulls his hand away in pain. He has cut his hand.*

EXT. INSIDE WILL'S CAR. OUTSIDE THE SORTING STATION. NIGHT

Oana is using Will's vanity mirror to repair her face.

OANA

So, you clean this area up, is that the plan?

WILL

Not exactly –

OANA

If you work with nature, why are you so against nature?

WILL

Well, a) I'm not, and b) I'm absolutely not.

OANA

The fox in your garden.

WILL

What about the fox in my garden?

OANA

The one wild thing in your life and it makes you crazy. Go
ahead! Turn the whole world into a park. Like Disneyland.

46

WILL

That's not what we do. That's ironic, because that's the opposite of what we do.

OANA

(*over him*)

Go ahead. Clean up! We will move to another alley and take the foxes with us. This is the human heart. This is the world. Light and Dark.

WILL

They put in Fortune Cookies now, do they, with the crack? This is the world. This is the human heart. This is shit. I'm sorry, but you just talk shit.

OANA

I have to charge you.

WILL

Yeah. Absolutely.

OANA

(*quite serious*)

No, I have to charge you. You crossed the line. We have chitchat. It's free. I keep warm. I buy coffee. It's a trade. You abuse me. That's business. Men abuse me. I get paid. Fifty pounds.

WILL

No way I'm giving you fifty pounds.

OANA

Fifty pounds.

WILL

I'm not giving you fifty pounds.

OANA

Fifty pounds!

WILL

No! (*Suddenly distracted.*) Fuck!

Miro is walking over the apex of the roof and looking to enter the building from the top window of its façade.

> OANA
> *(seeing the figure)*
> He's like a monkey.

> WILL
> *(thinks)*
> I should call the police.

> OANA
> To say what?

> WILL
> *(dialling)*
> That there's a man breaking into my building!

> OANA
> He's not a man, he's a boy.

> WILL
> *(on the phone)*
> I've got a special thing, a code, 4-3 er . . . No I'm Hoff–
> Yes, I'm Hoff– Well, my partner's Hoffman – where am I?
> I'm in my car! I'm looking at him! 4-3 . . .

EXT. WINDOW ON FRONT ELEVATION OF THE SORTING STATION. NIGHT

Miro has taken off a boot and sock. He picks a hole in the sock for a thumb and puts it over his wound. Will can't believe what he's seeing. He yells out, getting out of the car.

> WILL
> Hey! Hey! Come here!

Miro looks down. He negotiates the façade of the building as Will runs towards it. Miro vaults over the fence leading to the canal. A second and he's gone. Will is beside himself, tries to get over the fence, can't, falls back against some trash cans, uses them as steps, hauls himself over, ripping his jacket. Disappears.

EXT. INSIDE WILL'S CAR. OUTSIDE THE SORTING STATION. NIGHT

Still inside Will's car, Oana watches as Will chases Miro over the canal. She slides into the driver's seat.

EXT. CRESCENT CLOSE TO THE SORTING STATION. NIGHT

Dragan and Zoran watch as two police cars, blue lights flashing, swerve past them. Dragan starts the engine.

> DRAGAN
>
> We're getting out of here.

> ZORAN
>
> What about Miro?

> DRAGAN
>
> What about Miro?

EXT. CANAL BEHIND THE SORTING STATION. NIGHT

Will lands roughly on the other side of the fence, sees Miro running over the bridge. Will pursues. Miro looks back.

EXT. CAMDEN. NIGHT

Miro crosses the busy streets of Camden. He looks around for Will but can't see him. However, Will spots him, and follows.

EXT. COUNCIL ESTATE. NIGHT

Will watches as Miro enters the estate. He follows.

EXT. AMIRA'S FLAT. STAIRWELL. NIGHT

Will comes up some stairs. A passage/hall, side open to the street. He's disorientated. He looks at the doors, tries to get his bearings from the street.

He hears somebody coming up the steps. Retreats into a stairwell. Waits. It's Amira. She passes him. Her face is familiar to him but he doesn't remember from where.

EXT. OUTSIDE AMIRA'S FLAT. NIGHT

Amira finds Miro slumped outside the front door.

MIRO

Forgot my keys.

AMIRA

What have you done to your hand? Are you bleeding? (*She takes his hand, switches to Bosnian.*) I need to put something on this. Did you fall?

MIRO

No.

AMIRA

One day you'll fall and break your neck.

MIRO
(*going inside*)

I didn't fall.

AMIRA
(*in Bosnian*)

This needs a stitch.

MIRO
(*as the door shuts*)
Why can't you do it, then? You're a tailor.

Will peers around the corner as they go inside. His mind racing. He walks to the door. There's a bell outside with a name plate – SIMIC – and a card advertising a tailoring service.

EXT. KING'S CROSS. NIGHT

Will is returning to the Sorting Station. He walks, pensive, past the night's debris. There's the area's second population: the lost, the drunk, the decadent, the homeless.

EXT. THE SORTING STATION. NIGHT

Will walks back towards the office. He looks at the space where his car had been parked. Confused.

INT. THE SORTING STATION. NIGHT

Will comes through. Sees Liv and Bea with Sandy. Liv's in a state of high anxiety. Bea runs towards him.

BEATRICE

Dad! Dad!

LIV

Oh, Will!

WILL

I'm too old to chase robbers.

She hugs him. Starts to cry.

What are you crying about?

SANDY

Will, where've you been? We've been worried sick.

WILL
(*to Bea*)
Why's Mummy crying? And why aren't you in bed? I almost caught him. The police weren't here so I followed him. I'm sure it's just a boy. What did the police do with my car?

SANDY

The police were here for about a minute.

WILL

Are you telling me somebody's stolen my car? My bag's in there. My wallet. My keys.

LIV

You mean you left your car open?

WILL

I was chasing a thief.

SANDY

You didn't get a look at this kid?

WILL

Not really.

EXT. KING'S CROSS. NIGHT

Liv is driving Will home. Will turns to look at Bea. She's fallen asleep in the back.

>   WILL
> Reminds me of when I first met you. Driving around at night, getting her to sleep. You in your dressing gown. So beautiful.

>   LIV
> Will, a boy can still stab you. What if you'd caught up with him?

>   WILL
> I don't know. Anyway, he's not going to come back, it's probably all over.

EXT. COUNCIL ESTATE. SWISS COTTAGE. DAY

Miro and Zoran are training, using the slopes and obstacles of the estate. Will stands, watching them, unseen. Impossible to know what he thinks or feels.

EXT. COUNCIL ESTATE. SWISS COTTAGE. DAY

Will enters the estate. There's an iron gate, there are blocked-up windows, there are young guys in hoodies with dogs, there's trash. Not inviting.

EXT. OUTSIDE AMIRA'S FLAT. DAY

Amira's door. Will looks to knock then finds the bell. Amira opens, but there are security bars between them. Will carries his jacket.

>   WILL
> I telephoned earlier. About my jacket.

>   AMIRA
> Yes.

>   WILL
> This is strange, I know, because – you probably don't remember – we bumped into each other, the other day. Outside the Sports Centre. We gave you our towel.

                              AMIRA
                  (*still shy, not opening the security bars*)
That's right.

                              WILL
                        (*holding the evidence*)
So I've torn my jacket.

                              AMIRA
I can't repair that. I can, but you'd always see the tear.
I don't think – the cost – I don't think it's worth it.

                              WILL
Really? It's – it's a favourite, I'd hate to have to throw it
away.

She takes the jacket through the bars, inspects it more carefully.

                              AMIRA
I can try. Come back on Friday.

                              WILL
Friday. Great. That's great. I'll come back Friday. Great.

And she's shut the door. Will has no compass for what he's doing. He walks away.

EXT. COUNCIL ESTATE. SWISS COTTAGE. DAY

Will walks down the estate's long corridor. He hears a voice calling after him.

                              AMIRA
                          (*out of shot*)
Excuse me! Excuse me!

He turns. It's Amira running towards him. He's unsettled.

This was in your jacket.

She's breathless. She holds up a wallet.

                              WILL
Thank you. This is new. I've already lost one wallet this
week. Thank you so much. I'm an idiot.

AMIRA
(*referring to earlier*)

I was rude. I'm sorry. This city. See someone in one place and then in another place. Makes you –

WILL

Sure.

AMIRA

Working at home. (*A beat.*) I need to get back.

WILL

Right. Sure. Can you, if I were to bring a suit, can, I've lost some weight and I, if I brought it tomorrow, say? I live close by –

AMIRA

I'm out tomorrow.

WILL

Friday then.

AMIRA

Okay.

WILL

Okay. Excellent. (*Holds up his wallet.*) Thanks for this.

INT. FRANCIS HOUSE. BEDROOM. NIGHT

Will is trying on suits – the trousers are loose. Liv comes in.

LIV

She's asleep. Miracle. I can't believe it. Why are you trying on suits?

WILL

Nothing really fits me.

LIV

Looks fine. (*She's getting undressed.*) Can I say – Rosemary says?

WILL

Absolutely. What does Rosemary say?

LIV

Rosemary says – we know this – it's reinforcing. Bea says,
'I need,' I say, 'I'm here,' she says, 'I need,' I say, 'I'm here.'
I don't mean go to work tomorrow, I mean start thinking
about going back to work.

WILL

Good.

LIV

And start thinking about you.

WILL
(*it's so hard for them*)
Bea can come with me sometimes. She can dig. Make a
mess.

LIV

Great. But you're busy. And distracted. And –

WILL

And? Go on. And what? And she's not my daughter and
right now, when she's such, when she's so – you can't trust
me to take care of her.

LIV

If you were measuring, how far away, from where we need
to be, you and me, is that a long way?

WILL

I don't think you can really ask that question, it's not –

LIV

Put on a suit, sound like a suit.

WILL
(*taking off his suit*)
It feels a long, long way, right now, from where we need to
be. I wish we could unsay and unhurt back to wherever that
is, start again.

LIV

How far back?

WILL

I remember you bit me. You were angry with me. And you bit me. Don't remember why.

LIV

I don't remember why. I just remember I bit you.

WILL

You really bit me. And I thought we were very close. We were.

Liv is almost naked. So is he. She takes his arm. Bites it.

Yeah, but that's just teeth.

INT. AMIRA'S FLAT. DAY

Amira bites at a thread. A repaired jacket. Fine stitches almost conceal the tear.

WILL

That's astonishing.

AMIRA

It's not invisible, but –

WILL

Really, it's amazing. (*Gestures to his suit.*) Should I put that on? Is there somewhere?

AMIRA

My son's room. Just there.

WILL

I'm not –?

AMIRA

No, he's at school.

Will collects up the suit. Heads for the bedroom.

INT. MIRO'S BEDROOM. DAY

The first thing that Will sees are his architecture books. Then the little figures. His adrenalin surges. He touches the figures . . .

WILL

Is your son training to be an architect?

AMIRA
(*out of shot*)
He's only fifteen. It's a school project.

INT. AMIRA'S FLAT. DAY

He comes through, struck by Amira. There is something so passionate about her, behind the shyness. Will feels it.

WILL

I'm an architect, actually. Of sorts. Funny. Your son's project. We use those figures. The scale figures. They're from Japan. Hard to find in London.

AMIRA
(*professional, chalk, pins*)
He must get them from school. Raise your arms. You have children? You were with a girl.

WILL

My daughter.

AMIRA

I remember her. This will take a week. At least. I'll have to remove the lining and –

WILL

That's fine.

AMIRA

I'll write out a bill for the jacket. Should I just write 'repairs'?

She goes to a drawer, pulls stuff out to retrieve the bill. Including a folding practice keyboard. Will's intrigued.

WILL

What's that?

AMIRA

A practice keyboard. No room for a piano up here.

WILL
You should get an electric – you can get electronic
keyboards . . .

AMIRA
I'm happy with this. I imagine. Not a good place to make
noise.

WILL
You can always wear headphones. (*Looks at her.*) I'm fixing
this and it's not my business . . .

Will heads into Miro's room to change.

AMIRA
(*fingers to her ears*)
People like me, from my country, I'm Bosnian, we think it's
dangerous not to be able to hear.

He comes back into the room.

WILL
You should tell your son, if he's interested, to come and see
our office. (*Gives her a card.*) He can have a look round.
We're very close. King's Cross.

She looks at the card. Its distinctive logo.

AMIRA
I might do that. Will Francis? Is that your name?

EXT. COUNCIL ESTATE. STAIRWELL. NIGHT

Will walks down the stairs, pauses for a moment, carries on.

INT. AMIRA'S FLAT. DAY

*Amira is practising at her wooden keyboard. She is humming the tune
to herself. As she hums, the music becomes fully realised. This music
plays over:*

INT. PSYCHOLOGIST'S OFFICE. DAY

The music continues. Liv is crying. She wipes a tear from her eye.

> LIV
>
> That's our problem. She'll never be his daughter. I wish she was, I wish she was.

INT. FRANCIS HOUSE. BEA'S BEDROOM. NIGHT

Music continues. Will is sitting against the wall watching Bea and Liv, who are wrapped up in Bea's small bed. He turns off the light.

> LIV
> (*voice-over*)
>
> Then maybe we could all be happy. I don't want to be cold, I don't want to be sad. I don't want to be angry with him any more.

INT. BEDROOM, FRANCIS HOUSE. NIGHT

Music continues. Liv is sitting on the floor, soaking up the light that is pouring from her SAD light box.

EXT. BALCONY, AMIRA'S FLAT. DAY

Music continues. Will is on the balcony. Amira's been adjusting his suit jacket out here, evidence of her tailoring. His jacket currently has no sleeve. Will looks at the world going on, other balconies, other lives. Amira calls from inside.

> AMIRA
> (*out of shot*)
>
> Sugar?

> WILL
>
> Not for me.

> AMIRA
> (*out of shot*)
>
> I think you'll want sugar.

WILL
(*amused by the rhetoric*)
Okay.

She appears with a tray, Turkish coffee.

AMIRA
(*as she gives him a cup*)
Are you unhappy?

WILL
(*taken aback by her directness*)
No. I'm not unhappy. Why do you ask?

AMIRA
You always seem, when you come here, I don't know . . .
(*Shrugs.*)

WILL
I'm happy enough.

AMIRA
Happy enough? So English.

He laughs and sips his coffee.

INT. FRANCIS HOUSE. BEA'S BEDROOM. NIGHT

*Bea is practising on her beam. Liv is helping her, holding her legs,
encouraging her.*

LIV
(*voice-over*)
I think it was the happiest day, when Bea was born,
sometimes I think that Bea was punished. I left Sweden and
I left my husband. But then I met Will, and he was so kind.

INT. FRANCIS HOUSE. BEDROOM. NIGHT

*Music continues. Through the window, we see Will pacing out his
thoughts.*

LIV
(*voice-over*)
And we were happy, we really were.

INT. CORRIDOR OUTSIDE PSYCHOLOGIST'S OFFICE. DAY

Music continues. Liv says goodbye to Rosemary and walks down the corridor.

LIV
(*voice-over*)
But I just push him away. I don't know why. I just push him away from me.

Music ends.

EXT. OUTSIDE AMIRA'S FLAT. DAY

Amira opens her door. It's Will. Amira looks surprised. She's wearing a coat.

WILL
This will sound very stupid. I forgot the shirt. I was going to bring a shirt for you to copy.

AMIRA
Oh. Right.

WILL
I could go back and get it.

AMIRA
Okay. Or perhaps when you come for the suit.

WILL
(*of his visit*)
This is a bad time.

AMIRA
Without the shirt?

WILL
Right. That doesn't make any sense, does it?

AMIRA

I have to go to the supermarket, then I have to go to work.

WILL

Right. Okay.

He turns. Then turns back.

How do you get your shopping home?

AMIRA

Bus.

WILL

I'm practically driving a bus. My car is stolen, so I have one
of our company vans. It's electric. We could walk faster,
pedestrians will overtake us. Say yes – what's the worst
thing that can happen?

INT. SUPERMARKET. DAY

Will and Amira shop. She pushes the trolley.

WILL

Tell me about your son . . .

AMIRA

Mirsad.

WILL
(*contemplating its strangeness*)

Mirsad.

AMIRA

He hates his name. It was a name for Sarajevo but not for
London. Now he's Miro. But he should love his name.
Names in my country. They're like flags. You can live or die
because of your name. Mirsad, it's a Muslim name. He
should have a Serb name because of his father. But I'm,
I can be stubborn.

WILL

You can be what?

AMIRA

Stubborn.

INT. COFFEE SHOP, RAILWAY STATION. DAY

Miro is in a station coffee shop. He's working with the laptop. He's on line. He's looking at documentary footage of Sarajevo: soldiers in balaclavas; explosions; people screaming. He finds a photograph of a man standing by the ruin of the bridge. Zooms in: his father. Over this:

AMIRA
(*out of shot*)
When we were getting out, on the convoy – we came out with the Red Cross, leaving the siege – they asked his name at the checkpoint, the Serbs, and he said 'Mirsad'. If he'd said his family name, Simic, the Serbs might have shot him as the son of a traitor.

INT. SUPERMARKET. DAY

AMIRA
He didn't speak after that. Bosnian. English. For years. And he's never really, I don't think he's ever really . . . He gets in trouble. That's another story. (*She laughs it off.*) I can't talk about siege in a supermarket.

EXT. NORTH LONDON STREET. DAY

The Green Effect van moving through traffic. Will drives.

WILL
We had a break-in. Several, actually. At our office.

He doesn't know where this is going. Amira glances at him, suddenly nervous.

Something gets smashed. Broken. I mean, not just the windows. But not all breaking is bad, is it? You break habits . . . Maybe, maybe before we repair the window, we should smash a few more. It's all I do, you see, in my job. I tidy up. There's a mess around buildings and we come in. Squeeze in bits of green like dressing, like lipstick, like pretty. Anyway, that's a roundabout way of saying – the shape of your mouth – I could probably draw it by heart. (*He looks at her.*) What are you thinking?

AMIRA
(*not harsh*)
I was thinking, it was a roundabout way of saying you're married, which I know. I was thinking, a Bosnian man would say less, would want more. They love to talk. They love talk, believe me, but talk for them is politics. Women, for them, is not talk.

WILL
Well, that's, that's crushing.

AMIRA
No. I didn't mean it bad.

INT. LEISURE CENTRE. CAFETERIA. DAY

Liv is standing in a corner of the café, completing a call. She walks back towards her little group. Girls and boys in athletic gear, Bea among them. And Bea's trainer, Paul. Something intimate between Liv and him.

LIV
Dad can't make it.

INT. FRANCIS HOUSE, BEDROOM. NIGHT

A video screen captures Bea's somersaults. Bounce bounce flip. The camera pans to Liv who's clapping, excited, then swings back up again to find Bea, who flips again, lands on the trampoline, bounces, slows. Makes a bow.

WILL
That's great. That stop there's very good.

Will is watching the video on the bedroom television screen. He's sitting

n the bed, Bea next to him. Liv comes in from the shower, towelling
er hair. Sits on the bed.

                    BEATRICE
    Again!

                    WILL
    Again.

                    LIV
    What do you think? Great, eh?

                    WILL
    Great.

He's got the remote, is rewinding.

    It's good, too, because the batteries are back in the remote.

He squeezes Bea, who shoves at him.

    It's a mystery how those batteries find their way home just
    when we need them. Big mystery.

The image begins again. Liv sits down next to them.

    Mystery two – how did you video this and be in the picture
    at the same time?

                    BEATRICE
    Paul was cameraman.

                    WILL
    Paul?

                    LIV
    Bea's trainer. You've met him a hundred times.

                    BEATRICE
    Paul loves Mum.

                    LIV
    Paul loves Bea.

                    WILL
    But does Paul love me?

INT. CAFE, OVERLOOKING CAMDEN HIGH STREET. DAY

Another day. Will and Amira in the café. They're arguing. Amira suddenly starts laughing at him, his seriousness.

EXT. HUNGERFORD FOOT BRIDGE, SOUTH BANK. DAY

Another day. Will on the Bridge with Amira, looking over the Thames.

> WILL
> If you could do anything right now, what would it be?

> AMIRA
> I have to get back. I have to work.

> WILL
> Come on.

> AMIRA
> Anything? I don't know. Change everything up until this moment. Not my son. Everything else.

> WILL
> I can't do that for you.

> AMIRA
> You didn't say what could you do? What would I do, is what you said, not what could you do.

> WILL
> What could I do?

> AMIRA
> Why? I don't understand.

> WILL
> I don't understand either.

> AMIRA
> *(hesitating)*
> If I had a magic wand, I don't know, persuade my son to come to Sarajevo with me. Start a new life. That would take a magic wand. And you – (*She turns to him, candid.*) If you could do anything right now, what would you do?

And he kisses her. And kisses her again. She's crying, immediately. He feels the tears, makes him open his eyes.

Sorry. I'm sorry.

WILL

I'm sorry.

INT. FRANCIS HOUSE. BEDROOM. NIGHT

Will comes into the bedroom. The fox howls. He goes to the window, opens it, scans for it, out there in the night.

EXT. BALCONY. AMIRA'S FLAT. MORNING

Amira looks out onto the estate. On the balcony opposite her she sees a man cradling a baby; next to him stands a little girl. Amira smiles.

INT. AMIRA'S FLAT. BEDROOM. DAY

Amira comes into the bedroom. Miro fast asleep.

AMIRA

Are you waking up? I've made *burek*!

MIRO

I can smell them.

She gets in beside him. He makes room. They both eat a pastry.

You're happy.

AMIRA

Is that so strange?

MIRO

Put on the telly – it might be on the news.

AMIRA

You're not so big I can't sit on you. We should go home this summer, to Sarajevo. I think you would love it. Tanja says there are flights for a few pounds.

MIRO

Maybe.

AMIRA

Your grandmother would cry for a week.

MIRO

Great.

That's already a victory. She kisses him, gets up, goes back towards the kitchen.

He gets up. Dips under his bed, pulls out a stolen digital video camera from the pizza box. Turns it on, starts filming, films his project model. Zooms in, straight onto Will's business card. He panics.

INT. AMIRA'S FLAT. DAY

Amira's at the stove, pulling out more of the pastries. Miro appears, a sweatshirt on over his shorts. Brandishing Will's business card, increasingly frantic.

MIRO

What's this?

AMIRA

Oh, I forgot. I put it in your room.

MIRO

Where did you get this?

AMIRA

It's a customer. I sewed his jacket. He's an architect.

MIRO

What?

AMIRA

He said you could go and look at his office. What's the matter?

MIRO

I have to go out. What did you say to him?

                         AMIRA
What do you mean?

                         MIRO
Did he go in my room?

                         AMIRA
No. Just to try on some trousers.

                         MIRO
Why do people have to go into my room!

                         AMIRA
Miro, he's a good man. He was just trying to help.

                         MIRO
You think everyone's good. No one's good.

He turns around, goes back into the bedroom.

      I am in such shit!

She follows him.

INT. AMIRA'S FLAT. BEDROOM. DAY

He walks in, careless now of his mother watching him. Pulls back his bed to reveal his laptop, boxes, shopping bags, all kinds of loot.

INT. AMIRA'S FLAT. DAY

Amira sits and watches as Miro shows her what is on Will's laptop: the Green Effect animation; Bea's gymnastics; the photographs. She can hardly look.

EXT. CARWASH. KING'S CROSS. LATE DAY

Miro and Zoran are valeting a car, washing the windows.

                         MIRO
She's taken back the laptop.

                         ZORAN
You what? That is so fucked up.

MIRO

She says they're friends.

ZORAN

That's like, 'Hello, my son did it. Lock him up!'

MIRO

She say she's going to talk to him. Do some sort of deal.

Zoran, mind racing, gets up, walks away towards the carwash hangar, where his father is working with some of the other Serbs. Miro, still kneeling, looks back as Zoran explains to them what's happened.

EXT. KING'S CROSS. DAY

In the centre of the construction of the new station. Workers swarming all over scaffolding. Will, hard-hatted, is up there with some of the Green Effect crew. A tremendous din. Wei Ping has a model. Joe has plans. Will is discussing the implications of the project's progress with a site foreman. In his element. Orit calls up to him.

ORIT

Will! A lady is looking for you!

Then he sees Amira watching him from the road. She wears a trench-coat, carries a satchel, looks adorable. Will says something to one of the crew, then climbs down to her. His laptop is in her bag. Amira's ready to return it, to fight with Will about why he's infiltrated her life.

EXT. STREET. KING'S CROSS. DAY

Amira and Will emerge from the fenced area of the project and they're pitched into the world – King's Cross, Euston Road. Amira suddenly confronts him.

AMIRA

What is it you want from me?

WILL

Nothing. What? I don't want anything.

AMIRA

Because you can't just walk into someone's life, knock on their door, kiss them, and – you can't do that.

WILL

I know. I know that. What's the matter?

AMIRA

Or use me to hurt someone else.

WILL

You mean Liv? That's the last thing I want. Believe me.

AMIRA

Promise me.

WILL

Promise you what? I promise you I'm not flirting. I know
what that is and this isn't it. If that's what you mean . . .?

They stare, marooned.

I can't talk any more. Can't we just go somewhere and not
talk, not talk for hours?

AMIRA
(*believes him, complex*)
I have a friend. She works. Perhaps she would lend us her
place. It's close to here. It's not a hotel. It's not a palace.

WILL

Call her.

EXT. UNDER ARCHES AT KING'S CROSS. DAY

*From inside a black cab, Will waits, watching as Amira approaches a
mobile catering van. Tanja is serving fried food to men in hard hats.
There's an exchange with Amira. Tanja glances over to Will, then
hands some keys to Amira.*

INT. TANJA'S FLAT, TOWER BLOCK. KING'S CROSS. DAY

*Astonishing views of the King's Cross project from the common areas
as Amira and Will let themselves into Tanja's flat in this desperately
neglected building. The flat is tiny but tender, trying to make something
soft out of something hard. Amira goes straight to a closet, starts
hunting, pulls out a sheet, pillowslips.*

71

Amira's taken off her coat. He takes off his. They remake the bed together. Silent during this. Shy. Now there's no impediment. They finish. Amira sits, starts to unbutton her blouse.

AMIRA

The clothes, the clothes under my clothes, they're not, I've always wanted to make something in silk –

She hangs her shirt over the lamp. Shivers.

I'm giving myself to you. I want it to be worth something.

WILL

What? What are you talking about? (*He's touched, misunderstands.*) Stop. Come here.

She comes over. He turns her around by the shoulders, undoes her bra. She's unzipped her skirt. It falls. He stays behind her, kneels to pull down her panties, rests his head against her back until she turns into him and gradually falls back onto the bed.

INT. TANJA'S FLAT. LATE DAY

Tanja stands over the bed. She has a digital camera. Will is asleep. Amira lies next to him, staring at Tanja.

AMIRA
(*whispering*)

No flash.

Tanja nods. Amira presses against Will. Then pulls down the sheet, kicking it off, exposing them both in their nakedness. Without turning to Tanja she nods that she's ready. Tanja looks down the lens. Clicks. Clicks again. Clicks again.

INT. TANJA'S FLAT. EVENING

It's dark. Will wakes up. Has no idea where he is. Amira's shirt still over the lamp. He hears voices. Quiet, Bosnian. Amira is in her trench-coat, smoking a cigarette with Tanja. Will sits up, pulling the sheets around him.

> AMIRA

Hi.

> WILL
> (*to Tanja*)

I never met someone before when I was already in their bed. I'm Will. Thank you.

> TANJA

I'm Tanja. Good to have a man in my bed. I hope it's contagious.

INT. TANJA'S FLAT. BATHROOM. AFTERNOON

Will carries his clothes into the bathroom to get dressed. He sits on the bath and looks around him. He is lost.

EXT. TANJA'S FLAT. HALLWAY. EVENING

Will is leaving. He walks down the stairs, leaning onto the railings for comfort, and is gone.

EXT. KING'S CROSS. EVENING

Will walks out onto the street. Passes the uncomfortable mix of progress and decadence. Sex shops. Loft conversions.

> BEATRICE
> (*out of shot*)

' "Don't kill the boy," brave Benoit said,
But Dai replied, "Why not?
I come from the Isle of Wight.
We eat young boys a lot." '

INT. FRANCIS HOUSE. BEA'S BEDROOM. NIGHT

Bea is reading in her bedroom. Liv beside her. Will appears.

> BEATRICE

'But secretly Dai had a heart,
He kept it in a jar.

He hadn't seen that jar for years,
He found it in his car.'

Will sits down beside them. Bea continues to read.

WILL

Wow. Great reading.

BEATRICE

That's not reading. That's knowing by heart.

WILL

There's a metaphor.

BEATRICE

Where?

WILL

To know by heart.

BEATRICE
(*continues reading*)
' "Forgive, forget and eat more jam,"
The jar said on the lid.
Dai ate some jam and thought a lot
And in the end he did.'

Will and Liv join in.

'Go home and be a better boy
Although sometimes it's tricky.
There is a moral to this tale,
Jam makes fingers sticky.'

EXT. COUNCIL ESTATE. NIGHT

*Miro and Zoran push boxes with Miro's loot into the back of the van.
Dragan supervises. Vlado gets out of the van.*

VLADO
(*in Bosnian*)
You're a monkey, be a wise monkey. Somebody asks you a
question, you know nothing, you see nothing, you hear
nothing.

MIRO

I'm not a monkey, but sure.

VLADO
(*in Bosnian*)
Your mother's Muslim. They have loose tongues. Are you
my brother's son, or your mother's? We'll find out.

Miro is irked by this. He nods, walks back towards his flat.

DRAGAN
(*in Bosnian*)
And you don't come to the carwash.

VLADO
(*in Bosnian*)
You don't come to our house. If the police find anything
we're all going to prison. Hurry up!

*Vlado watches him and Zoran disappear up the stairs. Amira is
returning home, sees him. He turns and simply gets back into the van.
Amira stops, knocks on the window. Vlado puts up a hand in greeting,
but makes no attempt to open his door and address her. Amira keeps
walking, then suddenly turns and runs back. She kicks the door panel.
A torrent of invective in Bosnian. Vlado pushes down the locks.
Laughs at her. She kicks and kicks at the van.*

EXT. AMIRA'S FLAT. NIGHT

*Amira enters, the front door is ajar. Zoran is just leaving. He has a
bag over his shoulder.*

AMIRA
(*to Zoran*)
I don't want you in this house. Is that understood?

ZORAN

Whatever.

INT. AMIRA'S FLAT. NIGHT

*Amira takes off her coat. Puts the satchel with the laptop on the table.
Miro notices immediately.*

MIRO

Why didn't you give it back?

AMIRA

I will. I will.

MIRO

I don't get it. He knows, doesn't he, he knows I'm here –
why doesn't he just tell the police?

Amira looks at him, can't answer, then there's a scream.

INT. TANJA'S FLAT. AFTERNOON

*Amira screams, caught in a moment of uncontrolled ecstasy. A hand
goes to her mouth, she bites on it. Will's head appears. Amira's
breathless, intense.*

INT. SORTING STATION. DAY

Will at his desk. Sandy walks in, gives him a look.

SANDY

Will. You should come downstairs.

EXT. SORTING STATION. DAY

Will's car is outside. Will is confused.

SANDY

Just left here. The keys are inside.

*Will gets inside. Sits at the steering wheel. Turns on the CD player.
Oana's CD. He smiles. Now Sandy is confused. Will reaches over,
looks in the glove compartment. Fishes out a fox stole.*

What does that mean?

WILL

I don't know.

SANDY

Is something going on with you?

WILL

I don't know.

SANDY

Something's going on with me.

Will looks.

Erika. Erika forgave me. (*Shy.*) I mean, it's early doors but, you know, lattes have been drunk.

WILL

That's great. Sandy, can we drive somewhere? Can we drive somewhere now?

SANDY

Don't tell me you're fooling around, Will. I'm just entering fidelity, don't exit.

WILL

It's not about fooling around.

SANDY

It's always about fooling around.

Will looks at him. Picks up the stole, puppeting the fox. Barks at Sandy.

EXT. STREET. CHALK FARM. DAY

Miro walking, hood up, headphones in, sporting new trainers. A moped appears and falls in alongside him. Miro glances over, scowls, walks faster. Then starts to jog, then suddenly darts down an alley. The moped bumps up onto the pavement, follows down the alley.

EXT. ALLEY, CHALK FARM. DAY

The moped corners Miro at the bottom of the alley and stops. The rider throws Miro another helmet. It is Detective Bruno Fella.

BRUNO

Where do you think you're going? Get on the back.

MIRO

I'm late for school.

BRUNO

You're about two years late. You're in a lot of trouble, son.
Get on, put on the helmet. Makes you invisible.

Reluctant, Miro puts on the helmet, clambers on.

And don't stab me when we're driving. You'll fall off.

The moped weaves through traffic.

EXT. ALEXANDRA PALACE, NORTH LONDON. DAY

*A bench. The moped in evidence. Bruno sits, Miro won't sit. Kicks at
something.*

BRUNO

Everyone's running around looking for evidence. I just look
at the buildings and I know it's you, I know! Somebody's
doing very well, you're not – what have you made? A few
quid, pair of trainers? You're the bit you spit out, to your
friends, whoever they are. I know who they are, and they're
not your friends.

MIRO

How long are we staying here?

BRUNO

Ah, this is lovely. They should tip London on its side and
let a few million people slide off – there's no air.

Takes in an exaggerated breath.

There's no air in a cell. None. And that's where you're
going, no question. Unless you talk to me.

INT. TANJA'S FLAT. BATHROOM. AFTERNOON

*Will and Amira crouched in the bath, Will washing Amira's hair with
the rubber shower hose attached to the taps. They fool around. He
makes her laugh. He kisses her eyelids.*

AMIRA

Which of us is lying the most?

WILL

What?

AMIRA

That's not even the right question. Which of us is lying to themselves the most?

WILL

About what?

AMIRA

About this.

WILL

I'm not lying.

AMIRA

I have a photograph.

WILL

What photograph?

AMIRA

Of us. It's incriminating, is this the right word?

WILL

I don't know if it's the right word unless I know what you're talking about.

AMIRA

It took me a little while to make sense of the jacket . . . you suddenly appearing at my door. That you'd been following my son. You must know about mothers. They'd do anything to protect their children.

WILL

Why would you take a photograph? Was that why your friend came back? Why would you do that?

AMIRA

Why would you do this? You steal someone's heart. That's a real crime. And then what? You call the police?

WILL

No. I don't know. No.

AMIRA

Do you know how long since anybody touched me?

WILL

I should have told you. I should have said something. It wasn't a plan. It was you. That's the truth.

AMIRA

I have to get out.

WILL

Oh, I'm sure I'm guilty of that. So you come to bed with me. For what? A photograph. That's squalid.

AMIRA

(*she gets up, gets out*)

The water's cold.

WILL

It doesn't make sense. What about today? What about now? Look, a lie, that's right, that's me, that's my – I lie, I lie – but can't we draw a line, can't we say no more lies, between us, no more lies?

AMIRA

No. I have to ask you to lie. To continue to lie. I have to beg you not to report my son.

WILL

Is that what this is? A bribe?

AMIRA

If you like.

Will gets out of the bath now. Walks straight out.

INT. AMIRA'S FLAT. AFTERNOON

Miro, wearing school uniform, on his way back from school. He finds Zoran on the doorstep.

ZORAN

I'm not stopping. Old Bill was at our place. Says they're going to charge my dad.

MIRO

You shouldn't be here. What if they'd followed you? Then what?

ZORAN

You all right?

MIRO

Yeah.

He unbolts the cage. Zoran follows him in.

EXT. AMIRA'S BALCONY. LATE DAY

Zoran smokes a joint. Miro has changed.

ZORAN

They've been down the carwash, trying to make out they've got all this evidence. Trust me, they've got nothing.

Miro looks down, sees a couple of policemen coming along the long channel of the estate. Looks in the other direction. Four more. Stiffens.

MIRO

Zoran . . . my laptop! They'll find my laptop!

EXT. COUNCIL ESTATE. ROOFTOP. LATE DAY

And Miro and Zoran are running. Miro has the backpack with Will's laptop stuffed in it. He jumps a ledge. Zoran follows. Behind them, the police have made their way up onto the roof, struggling up the metal ladders. Another gap. They leap. Police coming in the other direction. Miro contemplates, then jumps off the roof. Zoran hesitates, then drops after him.

EXT. ENCLOSED STAIRWAY BY CANAL, AGAR GROVE. LATE DAY

The boys run over the top of the enclosed stairway. They run along the railway line, leaping each obstacle. Losing the police who call out for them to stop.

EXT. BRIDGE BY CANAL. LATE DAY

Miro and Zoran run across the bridge. Miro jumps up onto the ledge then drops from the bridge down to the canal walkway. Zoran is frightened. Jumps. Falls badly. Twists or breaks an ankle. Miro is thirty yards down the track. Stops. Sees Zoran is injured. Sees the police gaining ground. Makes a decision. Goes back towards Zoran, whose groans merge with the sound of women singing . . . a plaintive lament.

INT. BOSNIAN COMMUNITY CENTRE. NIGHT

A group of women, Amira among them, sing this nostalgic ballad from Sarajevo. Some of the older women dance, slow, proud. Two women come in, cropped hair, windcheaters, trainers (Erin Carter and Lorna Pearce). They approach the man on the door, ask for somebody by name. They look over. Amira watches them. They wait as she sings.

INT. HOLBORN POLICE STATION. NIGHT

The Bosnian song continues, haunting. A grim floor, processing the evening's drunks, vandals, thieves, gangsters. Erin and Lorna lead Amira into the noisy multinational chorus of complaint which accompanies the corridor of cells. There's a Youth Detention Cell. A small viewing flap. It's opened. Miro sits there, very small. Sees his mother.

EXT. ELEVATED PUBLIC SPACE, KING'S CROSS. DAY

A large elevated terrace, where Green Effect's work is close to being finished. Some ironic geometry in progress as the team map out a three-dimensional sketch of a large transparent structure which suggests a forest made of railway track. The work moving apace, lots of busy people. Will is setting Bea up at a table with paper and pastels.

WILL

Are you going to be okay? Show Mummy she can go and do her work and we can do ours.

BEATRICE

Okay.

He leaves her, passing Wei Ping.

> WILL
> Will you keep an eye on her?

*The two female officers, Lorna and Erin, appear with Bruno and
Sandy. Erin carries the satchel containing his laptop. Will sees them,
immediately apprehensive.*

> BRUNO
> Will. Some of my colleagues from the Youth Offenders
> Team. PC Carter, Erin, PC Pearce, Lorna. This is Mr
> Francis.

> WILL
> Will. Hello.

> BRUNO
> So, a fair result all round on the burglaries. DNA match
> and retrieval of stolen goods.

> WILL
> Sandy tells me it's a young boy.

> BRUNO
> Yeah, he's fifteen, he's been in a lot of trouble, he's had his
> final warning.

> SANDY
> He's going to prison.

> BRUNO
> If he's convicted, yeah, he'll go to a Youth Detention
> Centre.

> ERIN
> *(producing the laptop)*
> Is this your computer, Will?

> SANDY
> Got all your files on it.

> WILL
> Then it must be mine. Great.

Erin takes it back. Will is so uncomfortable.

ERIN

We'll have to hold on to it – until the case comes to court.

Bea has wandered away from her drawing. She's discovered an inviting stack of plastic tubes. Will looks over.

WILL

Bea! Wei Ping! Bea, stay with Wei Ping . . .

Bea is climbing on the pipes. Nobody's watching, all engrossed in the police deputation.

BRUNO

It's a hollow victory for us, right, Erin? Right, Lorna? Because the boy's just a little runt who does the dirty work – we can't make a case against the adults, the real villains.

LORNA

It's hollow.

SANDY

You might find it hollow. We find it whatever is the opposite of hollow.

ERIN

Of course. We understand.

SANDY

It's been a real siege. We've felt under siege. Plus innocent people were wrongly accused. Our cleaners. It's very degrading.

BRUNO

Because we know the boy, that's all. Nothing wrong with him.

SANDY

Except he's a thief. That's what's wrong with him.

BRUNO

No question.

SANDY
(*to Will*)

This is about – Will – this is about some kind of court –

ERIN

It's not a court.

SANDY

– a conciliation court? Right? We agree to meet this boy in court and – you'd better explain. This is a Camden thing.

ERIN

Mr Hoffman is right, sir, it's not exactly a court, but we work, this team we work with, the Youth Offenders team, we encourage offenders to face their victims.

SANDY

So, we show up at this court, sorry not court, whatever it is, and he might not go to prison?

ERIN

That's right.

SANDY

The law is an ass.

BRUNO

He's a boy, that's all we're saying. I know him. We all know him. Prison is the last thing he needs.

ERIN

You know he's a Bosnian boy. And his mum, well, his mum's in pieces.

BRUNO

What do you think, Mr Francis, you're very quiet?

WILL

I'd like to draw a line under the whole thing.

Wei Ping looks up at Bea, who has climbed to the very top of the stack of plastic pipes. It suddenly starts to give way.

(*Looking over.*) BEA!

The pipes collapse, some of them bouncing over the edge of the parapet. Bea disappears. Everybody runs, Will charging, his legs barely stable with terror, towards the ledge. Somebody reaches the parapet.

RUBY

Somebody call an ambulance!

Bea has broken her fall and is wedged between a cluster of pipes. Will reaches her.

WILL

Oh Bea, oh Bea, oh Bea.

WEI PING
(*arriving*)

I'm sorry. She just – I was distracted for second and –

Will cradles Beatrice, who's in mild shock.

BEATRICE

My leg hurts. My leg hurts.

WILL

I'm sorry. I'm sorry.

Will starts to cry. As if everything were broken, not just Bea's leg.

INT. CHILDREN'S WARD, HOSPITAL. LATE DAY

Liv arrives. Pent up. Ignores Will's look and goes straight to Bea, who's sitting up in bed, grimly cheerful.

BEATRICE

My fibula's broken. Two places.

LIV

Ouch.

BEATRICE

And they have to put wires in to fix it.

WILL
(*prompting*)

But the doctor said what?

BEATRICE
She said I'll be up again and climbing in no time.

WILL
We've got the X-ray, if you want to see –

LIV
Definitely.

BEATRICE
Sorry.

LIV
Oh sweetie, don't be sorry. I'm sorry.

WILL
I'm sorriest.

BEATRICE
Daddy cried.

WILL
I did not. I just laughed on the wrong side of my face.

LIV
Is it hurting?

BEATRICE
It did.

WILL
We've had painkillers. Bea had two and I had four.

BEATRICE
You did not!

LIV
Mummy's going to stay over. (*Pulling stuff out of a basket.*)
And I've brought everything, I've brought Stuffy . . .

WILL
Yes, this hospital is very peculiar. They don't understand
about colour – tried to put us in a yellow room!

BEATRICE
I need to speak to Mummy.

LIV

Mummy's here.

BEATRICE

I need to speak to Mummy by myself.

WILL

Okay.

INT. OUTSIDE CHILDREN'S WARD, HOSPITAL. LATE DAY

Will comes outside. He turns on his cellphone. Four missed calls. He recognises the number. He listens to his Voicemail, looking through the window onto the ward, Liv on the bed, cuddling Bea, listening to her.

AMIRA
(*voice-over*)

Hello, Will. It's Amira. Can you please call me on my mobile phone, please.

Will listens. Next message. Amira again.

EXT. PRIMROSE HILL. DUSK

The very top of Primrose Hill. Will walks up the slope, sees Amira in silhouette standing by a bench, London around her, twinkling. She sees him. Goes to meet him.

WILL

I'm sorry.

AMIRA
(*holding out a smartcard*)

First of all, I want to give you this, which are the pictures.

WILL

I wish they hadn't caught him. I wish I hadn't hurt you. Truly.

AMIRA

Then help me. Help him.

WILL

I can't.

88

AMIRA

This meeting, with Miro and the police. If you came . . .

WILL

I really can't.

AMIRA

He'll go to prison. He's agreed, Miro, if you help him, he'll come back with me to Sarajevo. He won't say anything in court except he's sorry. I promise you.

She places her hands underneath his top, feels his bare stomach.

WILL

Don't do that. Don't do that. I can't help you. Amira, how can I? If I help your son it will all come out. That I know you, how I know you. I can't. I'm sorry. I've tried – they've got too much evidence. They've got my laptop. I can't . . .

AMIRA

Please! Please! I beg you. I beg you.

But he does walk away. She watches him.

INT. FRANCIS HOUSE. LOUNGE ROOM. NIGHT

On a computer: the photographs of Amira and Will in bed. Will zooms in on them until they're abstractions. He deletes them. He sits and stares at the blank screen.

INT. FRANCIS HOUSE. BATHROOM. NIGHT

Will comes in. Liv's in the bath in this beautiful and sterile bathroom. A million miles from the one in Tanja's bedsit. Bath in the middle of the room. Walk-in shower. Will is stuck somewhere between these two bathrooms and the women in them.

LIV

I was determined not to blame you. I know it's not your fault, I knew it wasn't this afternoon, I'm sorry, I'm sorry, I'm sorry.

WILL

No, it's me who should be saying sorry. I've been looking for love, out there, I thought I might have found it.

LIV

And did you?

WILL

I think I might have lost the love I did have, the love of my life. Did I? (*Pause.*) Liv, I need to tell you everything. I need to tell you what I've done.

INT. CAMDEN TOWN HALL. COMMUNITY CENTRE. DAY

A small community centre. A busy lobby. Many events. Amira sits with Miro, jacket and tie, outside the main hall. Each time somebody new appears in the corridor, they look up anxiously.

INT./EXT. FRANCIS HOUSE AND GARDEN. DAY

Will is in the garden. He sits by the side of the canal, deep in thought. Liv watches him from the drawing room.

EXT. FRANCIS HOUSE. GARDEN. DAY

Liv approaches Will. He doesn't turn around.

LIV

I thought you were going.

WILL

I can't go. I slept with her. It was hard enough to tell you last night. That's bad enough without it being public, without hurting you twice.

LIV

When you hurt this much you can't be hurt twice. (*Trying so hard.*) I was looking at you, and then I was thinking how long it was since I looked at you.

WILL

I don't even know how to be honest, to be honest. Maybe that's why I like metaphors. Because I want to say there's a

circle, yours and Bea's, and I'm not in it. But that's just to
justify. Because there's a part of me, so dark, sees the circle
as a cage.

INT. CAMDEN TOWN HALL. COMMUNITY CENTRE. DAY

*Amira gets up, goes to where Bruno and the others (Erin, Lorna,
Legge) are gathered. They're talking to some other officials, one of
whom is a Mediator, who carries several files of documents. He has
looked over several times at Miro, his expression curt and severe. He
walks away, past Miro, and into the Court Room. Bruno watches this,
then turns to Amira. Amira nods, goes to the bench, collects Miro, and
enters the Court. Then the main door opens. Sandy enters. Then Liv.
Then Will. Bruno goes over to greet them.*

INT. CAMDEN TOWN HALL. CONCILIATION MEETING. DAY

*An actual courtroom but rearranged informally. A table, chairs ranged
opposite each other – for victim, for accused. Amira and Miro already
sitting. The door opens. Will, Liv and entourage file in. Many first
meetings, not least Will with Miro, Liv with Amira. The air thick with
feeling. Muted introductions from Bruno, then Erin sits opposite the
Mediator. During Erin's introductory statement, which she reads, Will
looks at Miro, looks at Amira.*

ERIN
So great you could come. If you could just take a seat here
then we can start –

WILL
(*interrupting*)
I think there's been some sort of mistake . . .

MEDIATOR
Mistake?

WILL
No, I mean, this boy is definitely not the burglar. (*Off the
confusion.*) I know this boy, and his mother, and –

LEGGE
What do you mean you know them?

WILL

In fact, they've been to the office, to our office.

Miro doesn't know what's happening. Nor do Sandy or Amira.

LEGGE

How can that be? You were told their names and you gave no indication of having recognised them.

WILL

I'm certain I didn't hear Simic. Did you say Simic? Amira and I know each other, actually quite well, and Miro is interested in architecture.

MEDIATOR

Mrs Simic?

AMIRA

He is, yes.

MEDIATOR

No, I'm asking is it true you and Mr Francis are friends?

AMIRA

Mr Francis is, I've done some work for him. Adjusting a suit.

WILL

I think, this is . . . Mrs Simic is trying to be discreet.

MEDIATOR

Discreet?

WILL

About the exact nature of our relationship. Which was not an appropriate one. I think she's trying to spare me some embarrassment. And my family.

He lets this hang. Sandy is boggled.

Which is probably why she's forgotten she's been to my office and that Miro came with her. I remember it well because it was on the day of the last burglary and Miro cut his hand. (*To Bruno.*) Which is probably where the DNA confusion comes from.

MEDIATOR

Mr Hoffman, do you know anything about this?

SANDY
(*shrugs, confused*)

I can't say I do, no.

LEGGE

I'm sorry but is this some sort of, are we supposed to be –?

LIV

Actually I met them both in the office. And I dressed the
boy's cut. (*To Amira.*) Didn't I?

Amira nods. She might weep. Will presses against Liv.

LEGGE
(*furious at the conviction disintegrating*)

No, no, wait a minute. We recovered a computer which you
claimed had been stolen.

WILL

Yeah, I lent Mrs Simic my laptop sometime when we were
together. She takes photographs and I was showing her
what to do with them, how to store them, how to delete
them. I'd completely forgotten. I was confused. Sorry.
Really sorry. It's absolutely my fault. Sorry.

EXT. CAMDEN TOWN HALL. COMMUNITY CENTRE. DAY

*The parties exit. Little families, Sandy, Will, Liv, the police, then Miro,
Amira. There are few words. Handshakes.*

INT. WILL'S CAR. CAMDEN. DAY

*Will and Liv drive away. He does a U-turn, they pass Amira and
Miro walking past the site where the Carwash is being pulled down.
Will tries not to look at them, turns to Liv. They drive on.*

WILL

What you did back there, you gave that boy back his life.

LIV

Stop the car.

WILL

What?

She's almost out of the car before he stops. She strides along the pavement, a torrent.

LIV

You don't get it. So that's it? Nothing happened? We just go home, right? Nothing happened! Go! Go to Bosnia!

WILL

Liv, what are you saying? Get back in the car.

LIV

Why were you looking for love? Ask yourself. Why weren't you looking for me?

WILL

Liv, get back in the car.

LIV

No! I don't want you in the house!

Will gets out of the car. Abandons it in the road.

WILL

You marry me then!

LIV

No! I don't want a husband. I want a good night's sleep.

WILL

Marry me. I'm so sorry. I want you back.

LIV

Then win me back.

WILL

How? How will I do it? I'll do anything.

LIV

I don't know. I don't know.

WILL

I love you! I'm sorry.

He pulls her to him. She jumps into his arms, wraps her legs around him, clinging to him, exhausted, desperate.

INT. THE SORTING STATION. DAY

Spring: a day with sun, a day when London shrugs off its ugly winter coat; enough of grey.

Miro waits in reception. There have been developments in this area of the building, not least the presence of flowers. In what was previously a glass conference room Liv has set up a small studio. She sits with headphones on, listening to something, making notes. Miro's eyes wander up to the rooflight, then he sees Will coming down the stairs.

                    WILL
Mirsad.

                    MIRO
Hello.

                    WILL
We didn't really meet. I'm Will. So you're off to Sarajevo? You wanted to say something?

There's a silence. Liv is watching.

                    MIRO
I wanted to say sorry.

                    WILL
               (*calling to Sandy*)
Sandy? Got a minute?

Sandy comes over and joins them. He is frosty, uneasy.

                    MIRO
I wanted to say sorry.

Will nods.

You know, and thanks for what you did. You've given me another chance.

                    SANDY
               (*shakes Miro's hand*)
Okay. Thanks for coming in.

95

Sandy goes back to his meeting.

> MIRO
> (*of the shopping bag*)
> This, I think, is stuff my mum mended for you.

> WILL
> Tell her thanks for mending stuff for me.

Liv watches through the glass, Will escorts Miro to the door.

> I thought your mother was going to come with you.

> MIRO
> She was, she's packing.

> WILL
> Sure.

EXT./INT. THE SORTING STATION. DAY

Everything has changed outside, too. The hoardings are down to reveal the canal and the housing project. All gleaming. The Sorting Station has softened somewhat around its entrance. A vine creeps up the façade.

Miro comes out of the building. Will emerges from the building to watch Miro walking away. He sees Amira waiting at the corner, as he sensed she was. Amira sees Will. A filament connects them. It's electric. And sad. Then Miro reaches her and mother and son turn away, her hand briefly touching his shoulder. Will turns and looks into his building, sees Liv.

Liv comes out of her studio. She is asking Joe how to use her dictaphone. Will smiles.

Will looks back at the street as Miro and Amira disappear, then heads towards his family.